Letters to my Friends
Words of Faith, Hope and Encouragement

PHILIP A. GUNTHER

First printing, September 2022
Second printing, July 2023

Letters to my Friends
Words of Faith, Hope and Encouragement

PHILIP A. GUNTHER

UNLESS OTHERWISE STATED ALL SCRIPTURE REFERENCES ARE TAKEN FROM:
The HOLY BIBLE, NEW INTERNATIONAL VERSION (NIV). Copyright 1973,1978,1984 by the International Bible Society. Used by permission of Zondervan. All rights reserved.

OTHER SCRIPTURE SOURCES:
The HOLY BIBLE, NEW INTERNATIONAL VERSION (NIV). Copyright 1973, 1978, 1984, 2011 by Biblica Inc. Used by permission. All rights reserved worldwide. Identified in text as NIV2.

Scripture quotations taken from the HOLY BIBLE, NEW LIVING TRANSLATION (NLT). Copyright 1996, 2004, 2007, 2013 by Tyndale House Foundation. Used by permission of Tyndale House Publishers, Inc., Carol Stream, Illinois 60188. All rights reserved.

Scripture quotations are taken from the NEW ENGLISH TRANSLATION (NET). Biblical Studies Press. 1996-2017. All rights reserved.

Scripture quotations are taken from the HOLY BIBLE, KING JAMES VERSION (KJV). Philadelphia, Pennsylvania: A.J. Holman Company, 1942. All rights reserved.

Scripture taken from THE MESSAGE (MSG). Copyright 1993, 1994, 1995, 1996, 2000, 2001, 2002. Used by permission of NavPress Publishing Group. All rights reserved.

Scripture taken from the COMPLETE JEWISH BIBLE (CJB). Copyright 1988 by David H. Stern. Jewish New Testament Publications, Inc., Clarksville, Maryland, USA. All rights reserved.

Scripture taken from the GOOD NEWS BIBLE (GNB): The Bible in Today's English Version. New York: American Bible Society. All rights reserved.

Scripture taken from the NEW ENGLISH BIBLE (NEB). Copyright 1961, 1970. Oxford University Press. All rights reserved.

Scripture taken from THE LIVING BIBLE (TLB). Copyright 1971. Tyndale House Foundation. Used by permission of Tyndale House Publishers, Inc., Carol Stream, Illinois 60188. All rights reserved.

LIBRARY AND ARCHIVES CANADA CATALOGUING IN PUBLICATION
Title: Letters to my friends : words of faith, hope and encouragement / Rev. Philip A. Gunther.
Names: Gunther, Philip A., author.
Description: Includes bibliographical references.
Identifiers: Canadiana 20220428948 | ISBN 9781894791571 (softcover)
Subjects: LCSH: Devotional literature. | LCSH: Christian life.
Classification: LCC BV4832.3 .G86 2022 | DDC 242—dc23

International Standard Book Number: 978-1-894791-57-1

FOREWORD

"Your love has given me great joy and encouragement, because you, brother, have refreshed the hearts of the saints."
Philemon 1:7

I met Phil Gunther some time ago when he was observing a workshop that I was co-leading. I drove Phil back to his hotel that day, stopping at a drug store to pick up pain meds for his nagging knee injury along the way. A good friend would have offered to run into the store and pick up the medication for him, saving Phil the unnecessary steps. But not me. I parked as far away from the entrance as possible, forcing poor Mr. Gunther to walk the distance on a bum knee. We chuckle about it now, but Phil must have scratched his head and grit his teeth at my lack of care over his condition.

My carelessness aside, Phil and I became fast friends that day. Phil is good at making friends. Mostly on account of his patience with and compassion for others. His chief concern is not himself but those around him. I know a lot of pastors—and this is not a contest, of course—but to me, Phil embodies the heart and character of a pastor. He relates to people with genuine concern and humbly speaks into their lives without pretense or hidden agenda. He's honest and transparent.

In the Spring of 2020, I was fortunate to be on the email list Phil began writing to every Monday. Each week I was blessed by his words of encouragement. I, like everyone else then and today, needed that encouragement badly. We were—are—living through a stormy season.

Phil's letters were too good not to share with a bigger audience of readers. Phil graciously permitted me to run his letters in the *MB Herald Digest*, where they have been warmly received. He continues to contribute to the magazine regularly, for which I am immensely grateful.

When Phil came to Kindred Productions to discuss the possibility of publishing his letters as a book, I was overjoyed. It's an honour to be a part of this project and to help share Phil's words of faith, hope and encouragement with others. Plus, it's the least I can do for making the poor guy walk that parking lot that day.

You're about to be blessed, dear reader: Phil Gunther wears his pastor's heart on his sleeve in *Letters to my Friends*. He does not hold back or sidestep his humanity or shortcomings. He is relatable, genuine and sincere, speaking to each of us as if we are his fast friends. Phil Gunther: big heart, bad knees. I'll take that any day.

With respect,
Carson Samson, Director of Communications, CCMBC

I owe a debt of gratitude to Carson Samson, Wendy Sawatzky and Vicki Clarke for their gracious investment of time editing and shaping the content of this work. Thank you to Janine Renee and my minstry executive team for blessing me with the time and space to write.

THE SIGNIFICANCE OF THE CROSS

Theologian and author Brennan Manning best articulates why I as a disciple of Jesus included images of the cross throughout this work:

"The signature of Jesus, the cross, is the ultimate expression of God's love for the world."

"The cross is both the symbol of our salvation and the pattern of our lives."

TABLE OF CONTENTS

Salutation   1

WEEK I
Letter One: God's Got You, and This   5
Letter Two: Life Under the Sun   13
Letter Three: Signposts   21
Letter Four: In Desperation, Deliverance   25
Letter Five: True Grit, Bungee Cords and Resiliency   29
Letter Six: A Light in Dark Times   37
Letter Seven: Sabbath   43

WEEK II
Letter Eight: Wholehearted   51
Letter Nine: From Devotions to DEVOTION   57
Letter Ten: Small, but Big   63
Letter Eleven: Gripe or Grow   71
Letter Twelve: A Cat, a Tree, a Lesson   77
Letter Thirteen: There Once was a Man   81
Letter Fourteen: Sabbath   85

WEEK III

Letter Fifteen: Hurry Up and Slow Down	93
Letter Sixteen: Hurry Sickness, My Fresh Insight	99
Letter Seventeen: Life Editing – Life Decluttering	103
Letter Eighteen: My Battle with 'Vertigo'	109
Letter Nineteen: Dad's Secret of Contentment	115
Letter Twenty: Contentment: The Path Less Travelled	121
Letter Twenty-One: Sabbath	127

WEEK IV

Letter Twenty-Two: Bold Benevolence	135
Letter Twenty-Three: Another's Troubles	141
Letter Twenty-Four: #blessedtobeablessing	147
Letter Twenty-Five: Ain't Jesus Somethin'	151
Letter Twenty-Six: A Life Poured Out	155
Letter Twenty-Seven: Of Visions and Dreams	159
Letter Twenty-Eight: Sabbath	165

WEEK V

Letter Twenty-Nine: Spiritual 'Mulligans'	173
Letter Thirty: "$3 Worth Of God" People	179
Letter Thirty-One: Uncommon Moments	185
Letter Thirty-Two: Safety Labels, Indiana Jones and Wisdom	191
Letter Thirty-Three: The Making of a Good Day	199
Letter Thirty-Four: God's 'Enoughness'	207
Letter Thirty-Five: Sabbath	213

WEEK VI

Letter Thirty-Six: Crooked Thinking	221
Letter Thirty-Seven: Dear Discouraged	227
Letter Thirty-Eight: My 'Stops and Starts'	233
Letter Thirty-Nine: Just One More	241
Letter Forty: ~~Just One More~~ One Too Many	249
Letter Forty-One: Good News People in Bad News Times	257
Letter Forty-Two: Sabbath	265

WEEK VII

Letter Forty-Three: Chasing Joy (Part One)	271
Letter Forty-Four: Chasing Joy (Part Two)	277
Letter Forty-Five: Chasing Joy (Part Three)	283
Letter Forty-Six: Chasing Joy (Part Four)	287
Letter Forty-Seven: Your 'Dash'	293
Letter Forty-Eight: About Looking Back	301
Letter Forty-Nine: Sabbath	307

Valediction	312
Notes	314

HOW TO BEST USE THIS BOOK

This book is divided into forty-nine letters. In every seventh letter a poem and prayer are shared. I encourage readers to read one letter a day, preferably starting on a Monday. In this way the poem and prayer are read on Sunday and could be used as part of one's Sabbath worship. Lastly, I invite readers to jot down their notes, applications, and conversations with God in the space provided under "reflections."

"Encourage one another daily."
Hebrews 3:13

"Encouragement is oxygen to the soul."
George Madison Adams

Salutation

SALUTATION

> "Beloved Friends, if this is how God loved us, we likewise ought to love one another."
> 1 John 4:11 CJB

It is with a profound sense of joy that I write. Hopefully I do so with the same spirit as the beloved disciple of Jesus, John. This pillar of the early church wrote his memorable words some sixty years after the resurrection of our Lord. In his epistle (letter), John addresses readers as "dear friends," a term of endearment, indeed. I am deeply attracted to this disciple's compassionate care for fellow believers. John's inspired counsel is pastoral; he encourages them to confess their sins, walk as Jesus walked, beware of anti-christs, see themselves as loved ones of the Father, lay down their lives for others, test the spirits and, perhaps of greatest import, love one another – "Dear friends, since God so loved us, we also ought to love one another" (1:9, 2:6,18; 3:1,16; 4:1,11). It is this inspired apostle's heart I wish to emulate in this work.

It was at the beginning of the 2020 COVID-19 pandemic when the Holy Spirit prompted me to start writing to ministry colleagues. In my journal I wrote the Spirit's word to me, "I simply want you to encourage them." For the record, I don't consider myself a writer, although I love writing. I also don't consider myself wise or imbued with a great pastoral heart. It is true that I am completing thirty years of pastoral ministry and along the way have learned a few things, but some would say I am still a bit too crusty and crotchety to be top tier. As for wisdom, I mostly stumbled into some through tough life experiences. The truth is, I attribute any sense of decent godly discernment to the Father granting my request for it.

All this being said, I wanted to be faithful and obedient to the Spirit's prompting and so each day I began jotting down what God was revealing. I then sent the following message on March 23, 2020 to ministry colleagues:

> *Good morning my friends,*
> *The SPIRIT moved me to send this email as each one of you is facing unprecedented challenges in your places of leadership. You are all servants called, gifted and loved by our LORD. He sees you, your circumstances and your needs. You are never alone, nor are you ever abandoned by our FATHER (Psalm 139). I will endeavor to daily hold you up before the ALMIGHTY.*
>
> *"Take strength from the grace of GOD which is*
> *ours in CHRIST JESUS." 2 Timothy 2:1 NEB*
> *"I don't bother telling GOD how big my problems are, I let my*
> *problems know how big my GOD is." [Unknown source]*
>
> *Blessings!*

Salutation

It was not long after sending this message when I began sending regular Monday emails to ministry partners. I shared the most pressing sentiment and reflection given to me by the Holy Spirit during the week with the cheerful salutation, "Good Monday morning my friends."

To make a long story short, God gave me other opportunities to share my journal musings for the purpose of encouraging fellow Jesus followers. When I was growing up my father and mother instilled in me the pressing necessity of encouraging others. They would counsel me that encouragement is a kindness that God expects of you. I pray that I have been found faithful to my parents' expectation.

This brings me to today. My friends (I hope it is okay to address you in this manner), over time, the maxim of King Solomon: "How good is a timely word" (Proverbs 15:23b) has come to deeply resonate with me. Likewise, the words of William Penn inspire me: "I expect to walk this life but once. Therefore, any good work, kindness, or service I can render to any person or animal, let me do it now. Let me not neglect or delay to do it, for I will not pass this way again."[4] This collective counsel guides me at the moment, and I pray that the words in these pages are genuinely a timely kindness.

Be blessed, my friends.

Letters to my Friends

WEEK I

LETTER ONE

God's Got You, and This

A SOVEREIGN GOD IN A CHALLENGING WORLD

> "...even there your hand will guide me,
> your right hand will hold me fast."
> Psalm 139:10

> "You do not need a great faith, but faith in a great God."
> James Hudson Taylor.

Hello Friends.

When the COVID-19 pandemic struck Saskatchewan in March of 2020, I went before the Lord and asked, "What is my anchor in all of this? What is the encouragement I can voice to others?" The Holy Spirit drew me to a psalm of David, Psalm 139.

In my life Psalm 139 has been a powerful word of hope and comfort. At the outset of the pandemic, fear, uncertainty and anxiety were gaining steam in the province and this psalm was a bulwark for me. I invite you to soak in the first ten verses of this psalm:

"You have searched me, Lord, and you know me. You know when I sit and when I rise; you perceive my thoughts from afar. You discern my going out and my lying down; you are familiar with all my ways. Before a word is on my tongue you, Lord, know it completely. You hem me in behind and before, and you lay your hand upon me. Such knowledge is too wonderful for me, too lofty for me to attain. Where can I go from your Spirit? Where can I flee from your presence? If I go up to the heavens, you are there; if I make my bed in the depths, you are there. If I rise on the wings of the dawn, if I settle on the far side of the sea, even there your hand will guide me, your right hand will hold me fast."

Slowly read verse ten again: "...even there your hand will guide me, your right hand will hold me fast." *Even there*. From these ancient, inspired words I was assured that the Father was present and sovereign in every and all circumstances. *Even there*, even in the throes of a pandemic I was in His grip.

Letter One

My dad, Peter, was a farmer, businessman and an ordained lay preacher. He was a godly saint, a servant of the Father. When I was a teenager, my dad preached a sermon about the sovereignty of God. To illustrate his sermon, he asked five young strong men in the church to come up on stage next to the pulpit. He instructed each of them to hold a dime using the non-pinching end of a wood clothes pin. They were to suspend that dime over a tin pie plate. During the first minute these men had broad smiles on their faces while they proudly held their dimes. By the second minute these same strapping stout men were beginning to struggle with their grip. The smiles disappeared. After minute three the men telegraphed nothing but worried and strained looks. By minute four, all the dimes had fallen, clanging loudly onto the tin pie plates. Somewhat deflated and certainly sheepish, these husky lads paid close attention to dad's application of this exercise. Dad's point was a simple one. Like these strong men who could not hold onto these dimes for more than a few minutes, there will come times in every disciple's life when they are unable to hold onto God. The good news, he proclaimed, was that God never loses His grip on them.

My friends, Scripture records: "I, your God, have a firm grip on you and I'm not letting go. I'm telling you, 'Don't panic'. I'm right here to help you" (Isaiah 41:13 MSG.). We will all encounter experiences that elicit fear, anxiety or despair. There may be a time when we lose our 'grip' on God through confusion, uncertainty, doubt or depression. It may come as a result of our own actions or those of another; either way it is simply a time when we can't hold on to faith or the Father. I know that space. I experienced it. It is deeply unsettling. During those times, remember that God has not lost His grip on us. He's always got us in His omnipotent right hand! And, He's always got our circumstances in His hand as well. He is sovereign over that broken relationship, lost job, injury or illness, failure or mistake.

Friends, remember the comforting hope that should encourage us: the future is in God's hands. Listen again to the Father's revelation: "I, your God, have a firm grip on you and I'm not letting go. I'm telling you, 'Don't panic'. I'm right here to help you." This word from the Father and my dad's sermon were significant factors in preparing me to face the pandemic and all the challenges it would bring.

Later, in the midst of the pandemic, God reminded me of His Sovereignty again, this time through nature. I was at a point of needing to catch my spiritual emotional breath. New infections were at their peak and emergency measures were put in place to stop the hospital ICUs from becoming overwhelmed. I longed for and needed another word of encouragement from the Father as I traveled to Canmore, Alberta with my wife Janine for our anniversary and a ministry sabbath.

From our B&B, I could see the picturesque snow-covered Three Sisters. They greeted me every morning. I was blessed. This trio of mountain peaks is a breath-taking natural proclamation of God's creative mind and omnipotence. These mammoth massifs whispered to me of ancient times and ageless things. Eons before I trod the rough, grass-lined pebble and moss pathways in this place, natural and supernatural life unfolded here with a grand interplay of sacred mystery and purposeful design. Long ago, it was truly an untouched space, a tangible declaration to the majesty of the Creator.

Today, this beautiful Canadian setting is less of an undiscovered country and yet, it still conveys a timeless message to my spirit, a word echoed by psalmists thousands of years past in a place thousands of miles from where I now stand:

> "Before the mountains were born or you brought forth the whole world, from everlasting to everlasting you are God" (Psalm 90:2).

> "I look up to the mountains – where does my help come from? My help comes from the Lord, the maker of heaven and earth"
> (Psalm 121:1).

As I gazed upon this wondrous creation of God, the Holy Spirit spoke to me through the following Scripture: "You will keep in perfect peace those whose minds are steadfast, because they trust in you. Trust in the Lord forever, for the Lord, the Lord himself, is the ROCK eternal" (Isaiah 26:3-4). Genuine peace was mine through simple faith in the Father, in His sovereignty.

On that trip, the Creator of the Three Sisters Mountains met me in a way that addressed my deepest needs. I was assured that the ROCK eternal was truly omnipotent, omniscient and omnipresent; a supernatural shield about me. In my experience of constant change and challenge, the timeless and permanent testimony of the Three Sisters remained strong and constant: God is; God knows; God helps. Nothing this world throws at me and nothing I do or do not do can alter this truth. In the beginning, God. In the present, God. In the end, God. Nesting this truth in my soul gave me peace beyond measure.

The magnificent mountain masterpiece of the Creator moved me to respond in bold faith. I worshipped with joy. I understood that regardless of the milieu in which I would find myself, or how I felt about the same, God is worthy to be praised and trusted. He is sovereign and more than able to work out for good all I could experience. The Three Sisters became my Ebenezer – my memorial of God's presence and power. My heart rejoiced: "The LORD lives! Praise be to my ROCK! Exalted be GOD my SAVIOR" (Psalm 18:46)! On that personal sabbath in Canmore my soul was reorientated from a space of disillusionment and overall spiritual weariness to one of trust, praise and joy.

When the pandemic struck Saskatchewan, I prayed for a word of encouragement. What I received was: God's got you, and this. At the height of the pandemic's fury, I again prayed for a word of encouragement. I received it once more: God's got you, and this. When I finally emerge from the pandemic and wonder "Where to from here?" I am convinced that the word of encouragement will be, God's got you, and this.

Be blessed, my friends.

Letter One

REFLECTIONS

Letters to my Friends

LETTER TWO

Life Under the Sun

IT'S FULL OF TROUBLES, BUT GOD STILL WORKS

"In this world you will have trouble. But take heart!
I have overcome the world!"
John 16:33

There is purpose in your pain, meaning in your suffering.
P. A. Gunther

We are problem souls in a troubled world, fallen creatures needing supernatural redemption by our Creator. Our sure hope comes from another realm, a kingdom far beyond this vast spinning sphere. Indeed, our earthen ark sails about a glorious sun, a celestial luminary in whose light we pray, "Our Father which art in heaven."
Pilgrimage Journals[1]

"More things are wrought by prayer than this world dreams of."
Alfred Tennyson, Idylls of the King

Hello friends.

No argument. 2020 was one for the books; 365 days that most just want to forget. Good riddance! It is telling that the most notable quotes of 2020 were: *"Wear a mask," "Flatten the curve," "Maintain physical distancing,"* and *"Wash your hands."*

My own sojourn through 2020 began with a heart-breaking closure of a church under my oversight followed by months of exasperating exchanges with former adherents. Then March arrived with COVID health and safety measures ending in-person church gatherings. My youngest son then contracted COVID in April and was incredibly ill for six weeks (and is still living with side-effects today). Supporting churches and pastors in their transition to online worship services brought a significant level of stress to my life during spring and summer. When the opportunity for rest came, our summer family vacation was cancelled due to COVID travel restrictions. Hopeful, Janine and I looked forward to a mini vacation in September only to arrive in Kelowna during a time when the California fires pushed choking smoke into this normally sunny and scenic Okanagan setting. As we moved into fall, COVID restrictions prevented us from attending our middle son's police college graduation. My year ended with a hemicolectomy. This surgery removed a section of my colon that harboured a large growth. Unfortunately, a complication developed and with it, significant anxiety. Six weeks of recovery followed. My physician ordered self-isolation meaning an in-person family Christmas could not take place. In the background was the potential for the pathology report to reveal if the removed growth from my colon was cancerous. When I submitted this writing, I was still waiting for my surgeon's prognosis. Friends, in a nutshell, my 2020 was a tale of trouble.

I feel I have good grounds to claim that 2020 was cursed. I postulate that the Apostle Paul would be in agreement since he wrote: "...all creation [is] subjected to God's curse" (Romans 8:20). This is simply life under the sun. Trouble is a part of every year and our sovereign Creator allows it. Job said, "Shall we accept good from God, and not trouble?" (2:10). Even Jesus counseled, "In this world you will have trouble" (John 16:33b). I recall a wise mentor advising me that life is fundamentally a sojourn of trouble and trial into which God pours grace, hope, love and joy. Based on this maxim, life under the sun will continue year after year until the end of days. The Preacher of Ecclesiastes seems to concur: "History merely repeats itself. It has been done before. Nothing under the sun is truly new" (1:9). The Preacher paints life under the sun as a protracted and perplexing crisis of faith in an enigmatic God. Life is the futility of human effort – a chasing after the wind – where meaning and purpose are as elusive as shifting shadows. A cycle of vanities that ultimately culminates in death.

In stark contrast, the gospel informs us that although all of creation lives under the sun, disciples of Christ experience that reality only in part. As Spirit-filled followers of Jesus, a new pilgrimage "under the Son" begins. We are now the beloved of a Heavenly Father

– forgiven, redeemed, possessing purpose and meaning – on a sojourn of hope that ultimately culminates into eternal life in heaven. The Apostle Paul pens, "For he has rescued us from the dominion of darkness and brought us into the kingdom of the Son he loves, in whom we have redemption, the forgiveness of sins…. This is the gospel that you heard and that has been proclaimed to every creature under heaven…" (Colossians 1:13-14,23b).

While I was in hospital in the fall of 2020, I experienced firsthand the contrast between "life under the sun" and "life under the Son." Like me, my hospital ward roommate (let's call him Lenny) had a surgery on his colon. Lenny was a retired senior in poor health and by all accounts and conversations, without hope in God. He had no love for 'religious' church people. He was living life solely under the sun. Post-surgery, both Lenny and I experienced exactly the same serious complication. We both had to work through incredibly anxious periods as we waited for relief. Throughout this time, I heard Lenny repeatedly use God's name in vain. He used harsh sentiments to express his great frustration with hospital staff. To be fair, he was hurting, and it was out of that pain he lashed out. He was living his trouble completely under the sun. Although I too suffered with anxiety and worry about my physical complication, as God's beloved I sought to rest my troubles with Him. I recognized that ultimately my life was under the Son, not under the sun. While Lenny used God's name in vain, I appealed to Him for help. While Lenny became agitated with hospital staff, I sought to encourage them.

They began to ask why I had such peace with my circumstances and why I had margin in my trouble to encourage them. I was able to hear the life stories of several nurses. The Holy Spirit then moved me to a greater compassion for Lenny. In obedience, I went to Lenny's bed, told him I was a pastor and that I knew his anxiety. I asked if he would allow me to pray for Him. I literally saw his countenance brighten and lighten. As I placed my hand on his shoulder, his frail frame relaxed. I prayed for him, at one point saying, "Father, I ask that you work good news in this circumstance."

When I returned to my bed, his doctor came in with a treatment plan that brought him hope, relieving him of his stress and worry. When the doctor left, I pulled back the screen separating our beds and said, "God heard us, Lenny." Lenny's face beamed the biggest smile since we met four days earlier. God touched Lenny's spirit and gave him a glimpse of life under the Son.

My journey as a disciple of Jesus over the years has impressed upon me that prayer is the primary means by which we "set our sights" and "think about" life under the Son. This is indirectly affirmed by Paul: "Since you have been raised to new life with Christ, set your sights on the realities of heaven, where Christ sits in the place of honor at God's right hand. Think about the things of heaven, not the things of earth. For you died to this life, and your real life is hidden with Christ in God" (Colossians 3:1-3). Prayer corrects human myopia transporting one in spirit to a reality we understand as the Kingdom of God. This kingdom is ruled by the One in whom "we live and move and have our being" (Acts 17:28). We pray in faith believing that our words supernaturally reach the Son who exists beyond life under the sun. On this matter, Julian of Norwich claimed, "Prayer unites the soul to God." More than that, prayer changes things under the sun. God ordains prayer not only as a means to relationship, but as a vehicle for personal transformation into Christlikeness. Even more, prayer impacts our circle of influence for good, and enables us to bear up well under our hardships; hence Scripture's passionate call to this spiritual discipline (Romans 12:12; Philippians 4:6; Colossians 4:2; 1 Thessalonians 5:17).

As you heed the call to prayer for the life and work of the kingdom, do so knowing that no matter what trouble comes – and it will come – Jesus promised, "In this world you will have trouble. But take heart! I have overcome the world!" (John 16:33). Indeed, grace, hope, peace and joy are our traveling companions as we traverse our lives under the sun.

Be blessed, my friends.

Letter Two

REFLECTIONS

Letters to my Friends

LETTER THREE

Signposts

NAVIGATING LIFE'S LANDSCAPE

"For now we see through a glass, darkly…"
1 Corinthians 13:12a

"We are never without a pilot – even when we do not know
which way to steer."
L.B. Cowman

Hello friends.

Not long ago my wife Janine and I took a sunny Sunday drive to Buffalo Pound Provincial Park. While traveling the winding roads alongside the lake, we came across a triangular yellow metal sign with a black arrow bent in the middle at a ninety-degree angle. This indicated a sharp left turn in the road up ahead. Below this sign was a smaller rectangular white sign with black letters that read "Keep Right." A moment of bewilderment ensued – should we go left or right? In the end we did successfully navigate the turn in the road while at the same time musing over the puzzling signpost.

Seemingly, these moments of bewilderment are now more commonplace in my life and ministry. Maybe this is due to aging or past disorienting experiences. Sometimes I feel drained navigating the tensions and contradictions that reach my desk, whether they be theological, political, philosophical, ecclesiastical or relational. Today, I resonate more than ever with Paul's words to the church in Corinth: *"For now we see through a glass darkly…."* Paul's assertion is a simple one; much of our sojourn in life, on this side of heaven, is one where ambiguity, rather than clarity, is the milieu.

Our world appears to be a complex and confusing place for any person to traverse. This reality is no different for the faithful disciple of Christ. In a world that too often declares right to be wrong and wrong to be right, evil to be good and good to be evil, how does one live for Jesus faithfully and with integrity? What is our counsel? What example do we set?

Letter Three

To help navigate this reality, my soul's map consists of several tested and true signposts. These markers help me traverse life's arduous or befuddling landscapes:

- Trust in God – *"Trust in the Lord with all your heart and lean not on your own understanding; in all your ways acknowledge him, and he will make your paths straight"* (Proverbs 3:5,6).
- Focus on Jesus – *"...let us run with perseverance the race marked out for us. Let us fix our eyes on Jesus"* (Hebrews 12:1b,2a).
- Anchor to Scripture – *"Your word is a lamp to my feet and a lamp for my path"* (Psalm 119:105).
- Listen for the Holy Spirit – *"But when he, the Spirit of truth, comes, he will guide you into all truth"* (John 16:13a).
- Ask godly counselors – *"Plans fail for lack of counsel, but with many advisors they succeed"* (Proverbs 15:22).

I match these signposts with my own personal experiences of God's work in my life – His love for me, His blessings and His faithful presence in all circumstances.

Today you may be at some kind of crossroad, perhaps struggling with a perplexing decision or torn between two divergent trails. Maybe the landscape before you appears dark, even frightening, and the way forward is far from certain. In my experience, the signposts I've listed above have proved over and over to be trustworthy and effective. They have given me that which I need to take the next step and the one after that and the one after that. And, where the path still remains uncertain I do what pleases God, I walk by faith (2 Corinthians 5:7; Hebrews 11:6).

Be blessed, my friends.

Letters to my Friends

REFLECTIONS

LETTER FOUR

In Desperation, Deliverance

AT THE END OF YOUR ROPE IS HOPE

"You're blessed when you're at the end of your rope.
With less of you there is more of God and his rule."
Matthew 5:3 MSG.

"God's address is at the end of your rope."
Dallas Willard

Hello friends.

In his Sermon on the mount Jesus teaches that the "poor in spirit" are blessed (Matthew 5:3). The Message Bible shapes it this way: "You're blessed when you're at the end of your rope." Jesus was speaking of people who understood their position before a holy and sovereign God. It describes a posture of the heart; a desperate awareness that one is spiritually bankrupt before God. The sense here is one of being at the end of one's rope and seeking God's help. Jesus says these humble souls receive God's approval and divine joy; they are blessed.

Jonah knew desperation. His failed attempt to flee God and reject a divine call landed him in a space he described as the *"depths of the grave"* and at the *"roots of the mountains."* It was from this place of darkness and hopelessness, where his life was ebbing away, that he remembered the Lord. He lifts a prayer to the temple of God, declaring that salvation comes from God (Jonah 2).

From within his living tomb, where the "earth barred [him] in forever," Jonah realized he could do nothing. It is here that a new faith seems to be born, a trust in God that is stripped of selfishness, self-centeredness and self-reliance. Makes one ponder – is genuine, God-pleasing faith, birthed out of desperation? Jonah's narrative points us in that direction.

And, perhaps Job's story also ushers one to a similar conclusion? After suffering devastating losses and crippling physical ailments, after arguing with God and His purposes, a new faith seems to spring forth: "My ears heard of you, but now my eyes have seen you" (Job 42:5).

Both Job and Jonah 'saw' the One who does not "reject a broken and repentant heart" (Psalm 51:17b); the One who is "close to the broken-hearted" and crushed (Psalm 34:18a).

Both Jonah and Job experienced despair, but deliverance sprang out of their place of desperation. Yes, deliverance from the dark realities of their immediate physical circumstances, but perhaps more importantly, deliverance from hearts, agendas and attributes that were more about themselves than God. Come to think of it, our own salvation from the devastating consequences of sin, which we were powerless to do anything about, fits here as well (Ephesians 2:1; Romans 5:6). Jesus was right, in desperation we can be truly blessed.

Be blessed, my friends.

Letters to my Friends

REFLECTIONS

LETTER FIVE

True Grit, Bungee Cords and Resiliency

MY DAD OFTEN TOLD ME, KEEP ON KEEPING ON

"Let us not become weary in doing good,
for at the proper time we will reap a harvest
if we do not give up."
Galatians 6:9

"Fall seven times, stand up eight."
Japanese Proverb

Hello friends.

The 2010 movie *True Grit* stars Jeff Bridges as the crotchety Rooster Cogburn. The drama's narrative follows Cogburn and his fiery sidekicks as they traverse the American wild west in order to track down an outlaw. During their pursuit, this spirited band faces personal demons, hardships and injuries. Their character, convictions and relationships are tested. The band's troubling experiences on this venture test their true grit. My favorite line from the movie occurs when Cogburn, after yet another failure, muses, *"Well, that didn't work out."* The statement was not resignation to defeat, but rather acceptance of reality in order to move forward – resilience.

Sometimes I feel like living life in our western culture is a real-life version of *True Grit* for disciples of Jesus. We are on mission in our own 'wild west' to bear witness of the Gospel. The challenges of being faithful in a culture that is hostile toward the church appears to be testing the mettle of virtually every facet of our spiritual formation and expression. We have often been frustrated, have faltered, failed and fallen. This season of the contagion has tested our true grit. Will we be resilient?

In his latest book, *Tempered Resilience* Tod Bolsinger defines resilience as, "...the capacity to remain steadfastly committed to wisely discerned goals and values when the forces in front of us and around us would seek to compromise both – and we become stronger through the challenge."[2] Resilience is having the ability to adapt to, and bounce back from, distressing experiences. It is the emotional strength to cope with trauma and adversity. Dr. Amit Sood, Executive Director of the Global Center for Resiliency and Well-Being, claims: "Resilience is the core strength you use to lift the load of life."[3] French philosopher Alain de Botton maintains, "A good half of the art of living is resilience."[4]

Bungee jumping has never ever interested me. The idea of jumping from a deathly height, entrusting my rescue to a cord of elastic strands, just seems, well, unwise. But that's just me. However, in spite of my hesitancy to trust a stretchy band to support me as I leap from the heights, I find the bungee cord useful as a metaphor for resilience. Individual elastic strands, braided together in some fashion and covered with a synthetic sheath, make up a bungee cord. Think of the bungee cord as resilience – the means by which a person bounces back from the possibility of destruction. In my life there are several key principles and practices (the elastic strands) that comprise my resiliency (the bungee cord). When someone or something throws me off a metaphorical precipice, it is these elastic strands – this bungee cord – that allows me to bounce back.

FOCUSING ON JESUS AND PRACTICING THE SPIRITUAL DISCIPLINES.

The first of these elastic strands is focusing on Jesus and practicing the spiritual disciplines like prayer, meditation and fasting. Spiritual disciplines are habits of devotion; they are the tangible vehicles which help us focus on Jesus. The author of Hebrews counsels disciples to fix their thoughts and eyes on Jesus, especially during times of trouble (Hebrews 3:1; 12:2). The apostle Paul instructs disciples facing hardship: "Set your minds on things above, not on earthly things" (Colossians 3:2). In short, we must look past ourselves and our troubles to the One who is our ROCK eternal and SAVIOUR. Resilient followers see hardship and suffering as an expected, if not integral, aspect of following Jesus. Resilience increases as we become Christocentric in our world view and approach to life, and create space in our lives to connect with Jesus. Richard Foster once wrote: "The disciplines allow us to place ourselves before God so that He can transform us."[5]

DEVELOPING SELF-AWARENESS AND SELFCARE

A second set of elastic strands are self-awareness and selfcare. As I navigated my personal quest to a deeper understanding of resilience, it quickly became apparent that in order for me to foster resiliency, I needed to do the deep and difficult work of self-examination. *"Nothing changes until we are brutally honest with the person in the mirror,"* writes Andy Stanley.[6] I believed that I couldn't bolster my resiliency if I did not know myself. What were my strengths weaknesses, inclinations and habits? What were my virtues and shadows? I needed to explore my emotional, physical, mental and spiritual wellbeing. It was also critical to assess my environmental contexts (work, family, recreation, stressors, etc.) to see how I was being impacted by them. From this over-arching inventory I was able to pinpoint what elements of my current life bolstered resiliency and those that undermined it. I sought to transform or eliminate the latter.

Once I better understood myself, I began to make incremental personal changes toward selfcare. One of the best outcomes of self-awareness and selfcare is that I seem to have a greater capacity to support others in their hardships. American anthropologist Eleanor Brownn stated, *"Selfcare is not selfish; you cannot serve from an empty vessel."*[7] Rabbi Dr. Jonathan Sacks writes, *"No one is stronger than the person who knows who and what he is."*[8]

I must add here that participation in a healthy community circle is an essential aspect of selfcare. Resilient people generally have solid support from family, friends and their faith community. Resilient people share their burdens and troubles, inviting counsel, prayer and hands-on help in other tangible ways. The church has a vital role to play in developing resilient disciples. In sum, resilient people know themselves and understand how to take care of themselves.

KNOWING ONE'S IDENTITY AND CALLING

Resilient individuals know "who" they are because they know "whose" they are. Identity and calling are my last set of elastic strands and are foundational pieces for resiliency. I understand that I am the beloved of the Heavenly Father – known, loved, forgiven, empowered, protected and made righteous. My calling is to be a disciple of Jesus; to live life in a manner that brings glory to

Him through worship, witness and service. A disciple who increasingly becomes like Him in thought, words and actions. Confidence in one's place and purpose provide the courage needed to bounce back from troubles.

How does knowing my identity and calling foster resiliency? My best response is to have you consider Viktor Emil Frankl's thoughts in *Man's Search For Meaning* (1959). His work has sold more than ten million copies worldwide and is listed as one of the top ten most influential books in the United States – a remarkable feat! Frankl was an Austrian Holocaust survivor whose father, mother and wife perished in German concentration camps. Frankl lived through perhaps the worst of human experiences in these Nazi camps of death. He was stripped of absolutely everything. Out of his experiences in this cauldron of evil, Frankl quoted German philosopher Fredrich W. Nietzsche, "Those who have a 'why' to live, can bear with almost any 'how'," and then surmised that without meaning and purpose in life, circumstances become overwhelming and life unbearable.[9] Other than the biblical Job, Frankl is perhaps one of the most resilient people that I can think of. His secret? He knew his identity and purpose (calling).

It has been said that, *"If you're going through hell, keep going."*[10] I am convinced that it is truly in the battle where tenacity is birthed and matured. A fundamental truth about resilience is that one is not born with it; one develops it. Resilience is all about surviving and thriving; it is in the thick of the fight where one is able to acquire the toughness to keep on keeping on.

My friends, resiliency in faith and life is not a fait

accompli. I am under construction on multiple levels and will continue to be so on this side of heaven. It is my prayer that you may be encouraged to test these findings in the lab of your own spiritual formation, adopting what fosters wellbeing and refining what falls short. May your true grit in hardship be like Christ in His own suffering and journey to the cross. May you be able to echo the words Apostle Paul: For I am already being poured out like a drink offering, and the time for my departure is near. I have fought the good fight, I have finished the race, I have kept the faith. Now there is in store for me the crown of righteousness, which the Lord, the righteous Judge, will award to me on that day—and not only to me, but also to all who have longed for his appearing" (2 Timothy 4:6-8). May your resilience be as flexible and strong as a bungee cord.

Be blessed, my friends.

Letters to my Friends

REFLECTIONS

LETTER SIX

A Light in Dark Times

LIGHT IS HOPE

"I have come into the world as a light,
so that no one who believes in me
should stay in darkness."
John 12:46

"Darkness cannot drive out darkness;
only light can do that."
Rev. Dr. Martin Luther King, Jr.

Hello friends.

In my younger days, I was an amateur SCUBA diver. My older brother and I relished freshwater diving, particularly in the depths of Cultus Lake near Chilliwack, B.C. Although we spent most of our time in the lake's shallower waters, sometimes we ventured to around 105 feet deep. Here the water was frigid, the lake bed was flat, limous and grey in colour, and it was dark. I still remember turning off my light and immediately feeling disoriented, unsafe and anxious. Fear instantly began welling up in my spirit and I had to quickly revert to my training and remain calm. I was so very thankful to have a light to pierce the darkness that surrounded me. The light brought definition to my circumstances, provided illumination to my course, safety from potential hazards and instilled hope that I would surface from the dive.

As disciples of Jesus, our lives can at times feel like we are on one of those deep dives with the flashlight turned off – disoriented, lonely, cold and unsafe. In one's chilling pitch-black experience, anxiety, worry, and then fear, soon extrude. The root cause for our darkness can be external or internal, simple or complex, long-standing or new. The source can be physical, mental, emotional or spiritual. It can be the result of our own choice or the decision of another. At the end of the day, whatever the reason for our trepidation, we just want light in the darkness.

JESUS IS THE LIGHT. JESUS IS YOUR LIGHT.

I love that the theme of light is threaded throughout

Scripture and points to God as its ultimate source. At creation, God speaks light into being and deems it good ("And God said, "Let there be light, and there was light..." Genesis 1:3). Inscribed in the middle of Scripture is King David's declaration, "The LORD is my light..." (Psalm 27:1a). God's word is a "light for [our] path" (Psalm 119:105b). "God is light," (1 John 1:5). And, at the end of days John writes, "There will be no more night. They will not need the light of a lamp or the light of the sun, for the Lord God will give them light..." (Revelation 22:5).

Between Genesis and Revelation, not only is light used to describe the work of Jesus, but he is also revealed as *the* Light. Note the following examples:

- *"The people walking in darkness have seen a great light..."* Speaking of the Messiah, Isaiah 9:2 and Matthew 4:16
- *"In him was life and that life was the light of all mankind. The light shines in the darkness, and darkness has not overcome it."* Speaking of the incarnation of Jesus, John 1:4,5
- *"I am the light of the world. Whoever follows me will never walk in darkness, but will have the light of life."* Jesus, John 8:12
- *"I have come into the world as a light, so that no one who believes in me should stay in darkness."* Jesus, John 12:46

As a disciple, I testify that because Jesus is my Light, He...

- ENLIGHTENS the path of my spiritual formation;
- ILLUMES my identity and purpose;
- ELUCIDATES my understanding of God and His will for my life;
- REVEALS my ungodly motivations, illuminating

the opaque recesses of my heart;
- EXPOSES the lies in my life that cause uncertainty, anxiety and fear;
- IS A BEACON of hope in seasons of my life that are dark; and
- BRINGS clarity to my circumstances and how to navigate them.

We are the light of Jesus. Light is in us.

In the 2015 issue of *Decision magazine* Anne Graham Lotz wrote,

"When the Scottish novelist Robert Louis Stevenson was a child, the story is told that one night his nanny came into his nursery to put him to bed. She found the little boy looking intently out of his bedroom window. When she called to him, he continued staring into the darkness, so she went over to ask him what he found so interesting outside. As she peered over his shoulder, she saw the lamplighter walking down the street, lighting the streetlamps. Little Robert responded, 'Look, Nanny. I'm watching as that man puts holes in the darkness.' "[11]

Some 1800 years before Robert Louis Stevenson is said to have uttered these insightful words, Jesus inspired his disciples by calling them to be those people who put holes in the darkness. Jesus said, "You are the light of the world...let your light shine before others." (Matthew 5:14&16). The Apostle Paul echoes this call for Jesus' disciples to be points of light in the world when he wrote to the church in Ephesus: "For you were once darkness, but now you are light in the Lord. Live

Letter Six

as children of light" (Ephesians 5:8). And also, to the church in Thessalonica: "You are all children of light" (1 Thessalonians 5:5).

As disciples, our privilege is to shine as *Jesus'* lights. In my journal I wrote:

> If Christ is genuinely Lord in our lives, we will be undeniably luminiferous, candescent souls beaming with the hope, peace and joy of the Savior. Ours is a mission to countervail darkness from whatever horrific abyss it climbs bent on destroying good and godly alike. We rise to this beseechment, not in our authority, but by the Lion of Judah's fiat. We are Christ's spiritually armoured foot soldiers dispelling and vanquishing the dark about us. And, unlike our spiritual adversaries, we accomplish our kingdom 'sorties' with gentleness, grace and love.[12]

As a Capernwray student in Australia, my wife Janine once went on a weekend adventure with her schoolmates spelunking (caving) at a nearby national park. At one point, the guide huddled everyone around telling them to shut off their headlamps. He told them that it would be incredibly dark, not to panic, and that he would ensure their safety. Her experience reminds me that as disciples, we are never alone in dark times and our divine guide is always with us lighting the way and, like this spelunking guide, we are to be guides (lights) for others who find themselves in the dark.

A final thought from L.B. Cowman; "We are safer with God in the dark than without him during the sunshine."[13]

Be blessed, my friends.

Letters to my Friends

REFLECTIONS

LETTER SEVEN

Sabbath

Letters to my Friends

Hello Friends.

I penned *Fragile* while visiting Ladysmith on Vancouver Island, British Columbia in the summer of 2011. This work came only days after I ruptured my Achilles tendon and was told I would be in an air cast with crutches for three months. The event reminded me of just how delicate my body is and how truly tenuous good health can be.

FRAGILE

I am discovering, Lord, just how fragile I am:
    brittle, broken, susceptible to fatigue and fracture.
My frame, divinely molded and God-breathed,
    is winding down, wearing out, wasting away.
Despite all efforts to nurture this living ash and dust,
    I am slowly returning from whence I came.
From the moment I was, my days were allotted, my years appointed;
    such is the nature of all things living.
All life is delicate, all creation tentative;
    each moment a blessing, each breath a gift.
Lord, I take these discoveries, these truths, to heart;
    not as burdens to bear but revelations to grasp.
In them is much for my soul,
    a rich bounty for my spirit.
For when I understand and accept that I am fragile,
    I am given a grace, an opportunity to depend upon you.
Lord, you become my help, healing and hope as I let go,
    as I release all my delusions of strength, control and power.
I accept that I am fragile,
    and in that discovery I am mysteriously made whole.

Letter Seven

For when I am weak, then, in you, I am made strong.*

**Heartwork – An Endless Hallelujah*, PG, 2011.

Letters to my Friends

SABBATH PRAYER

First Prayer was written during my pastoral sabbatical in the summer of 2011. This is my first prayer of the day.

"Pray continually."
1 Thessalonians 5:17

"Prayer is the oxygen of the soul."
St. Padre Pio

FIRST PRAYER

Holy, holy, holy, are you Lord God Almighty.
Sovereign – all knowing, all-powerful, present everywhere.
King of kings, Lord of lords, God of gods.
There is none who stands before you.
You are my Creator, my Redeemer, and my Sustainer.
In you I live and move and have my being.
All that I am and all that I am steward of, comes from your hand.
You are the Horn of my salvation, the Shield of my faith.
You are the Rock that is higher than I.
You are Light, Love and Life.
In all that you are and in all that you do, you are right and good.
Your loving-kindness is without fail.

I worship you.
I exalt you.
I praise you.

Letter Seven

Thank you for Jesus who died for my sins.
Thank you for your Holy Spirit who leads and guides me
    each day.
Thank you for your Word which is a lamp for my feet and a light
    for my path.
Thank you for my life.
Thank you for this new day and all the opportunities it holds.
Thank you for your love and grace.
Thank you for family and friends.
Thank you for your appointing and anointing on my life.
Thank you for your heavenly wisdom.
Thank you for daily bread, a safe home and Canada, a land of
    peace and prosperity.
To you, and you alone, I surrender my body, mind, soul, heart
    and spirit
without hesitation or reservation.
Amen.*

*Heartwork – An Endless Hallelujah, PG, 2011.

Letters to my Friends

REFLECTIONS

Letter Seven

WEEK II

Letters to my Friends

Letter Eight

LETTER EIGHT

Wholehearted

BEING ALL IN

"For Christ's love compels us...."
2 Corinthians 5:14a

"Hold back nothing of yourselves for yourselves
so that He who gives Himself totally to
you may receive you totally."
St. Francis of Assisi

Hello Friends.

Lately, I have been committing more of my devotional time to soaking in Jesus' words: "Love the Lord your God with all your heart and with all your soul and with all your mind and with all your strength" (Mark 12:29-30). I have pondered my own historical interaction and application of this command. I sense there is room for growth. As a disciple, do I genuinely understand this divine expectation upon my life? What is the source of 'all-in' godly living? What does living wholeheartedly ("all" of my heart, soul, mind and strength) look like? Does Scripture speak to the opposite of wholehearted discipleship and its consequences?

I am convinced that being a wholehearted disciple is a posture, a bearing, an attitude. It involves the way you understand, and respond to, God. It is both devotion and dedication. It is dynamic, organic and living. It requires an equal degree of saying yes and saying no — yes to those things that foster deeper adoration and commitment, and no to those things that undermine it.

Experience has taught me that people who live wholehearted lives as disciples of Jesus are difference-makers. Disciples who make an impact in their settings are all-in when it comes to their walk with Jesus and in their obedience to Him. They are not on the bench, but in the game, so-to-speak. They may not be charismatic or particularly skilled or even scholarly, but they show up, speak up and stand up for their faith. They are first in line to serve, believing that we are actually to walk as Jesus walked. Although they are often in the background,

Letter Eight

they are the banner bearers, flag wavers, cheerleaders, the sold-out ones.

So where then does wholehearted living originate? I am persuaded that true wholehearted living for God arises from our identity in Christ as being the beloved. Author Kyle Idleman in his book *Not a Fan* writes, "One of the greatest motivations of our love and passionate pursuit of Jesus is a better understanding of how great his love is for us. Being loved causes us to love."[14] Being wholehearted is a response to our grace status as adopted daughters and sons of the King, heirs to the promises of God. Scripture informs us that the love of Christ compels us (2 Corinthians 5:14-15), the sacrifice of Christ sets us on a new life path (Galatians 2:20) and the presence of the Holy Spirit sanctifies and empowers us on this sojourn (Romans 15:16). In short, genuine wholehearted living for God springs not from any religious efforts at appeasing Him, but from a recognition of, and response to, the gospel. It is because of God that we are redeemed; it is out of our gratitude for our redemption that we live as wholehearted disciples.

Is there an example of a believer who loved God wholeheartedly? For me, David comes to mind. God is recorded as saying of him: *"I have found David, son of Jesse a man after my own heart; he will do everything I want him to do"* (Acts 13:22). We all know that David's story is one of great successes and colossal moral failures. His transgressions resulted in adultery and murder. And yet, David remains an example of wholehearted devotion to God. Why? The answer appears within David's life narrative and embedded in his psalms:

- David had a genuine faith in God.
- David acted courageously out of his trust in God's sovereignty.
- David brought glory to God and honour to God's people.
- David worshipped God with authenticity.
- David loved God's law.
- David was humble before God.
- David was thankful to God.
- David confessed and repented of his sins.

David was not without flaws and failures; however, his whole heart was God-oriented. David's narrative shows that failing and being wholly God oriented are not mutually exclusive. We all have flaws and we all fall short, but we can still be wholehearted in our devotion to God.

The Scripture speaks unflatteringly of those who choose not to live for Jesus in a manner that is wholehearted. For example, Revelation speaks of the believers at Laodicea as being lukewarm. They were described as being neither hot nor cold when it came to the person and purposes of God (Revelation 3:14ff). These tepid posers are summarily spit out by God. As a disciple of Jesus do I want to be known as a half-hearted tag-along rather than a faithful, devoted, all-in for Jesus, believer? The seduction to lukewarm living is very real. In his book, *The Way of The Heart,* author Henri Nouwen writes, "It is not difficult to see that in this fearful and painful period of our history we are having a difficult time fulfilling our task of making the light of Christ shine into the darkness. Many of us have adapted ourselves too well to the general mood of lethargy."[15] Nouwen's sentiments

Letter Eight

are sobering. We must heed the counsel of Paul, "Never be lacking in zeal, but keep your spiritual fervor, serving the Lord" (Romans 12:11). In other words, remain wholehearted.

We must be more than enthusiastic admirers of Jesus. We must be about more than ending our tweets with #blessed or attaching WWJD stickers on our car windows. We must be about more than wearing a cross on a necklace or bearing a catchy Christian motto on a T-shirt. We must be deeper, louder and bolder for Jesus, not because of religious duty or aspirations of earning favour with God, but as a tangible response to His unfathomable love and grace. He loves us wholeheartedly; can we respond in kind?

Be blessed, my friends.

Letters to my Friends

REFLECTIONS

LETTER NINE

From Devotions to DEVOTION

FROM PRACTICE TO PRESENCE

"Where you go I will go...."
Ruth 1:16

"The main measure of your devotion to God is not your devotional life. It is simply your life."
John Ortberg

Hello Friends.

Doing devotions, that is reading Scripture and praying, has been ingrained in me since I first became a believer. This practice has proven to be incredibly edifying and life-transforming. I commend this spiritual discipline without reservation to those I am discipling. However, I also instill in them that unless their daily devotions translate into a lifestyle of devotion, they have missed the point of the exercise. Doing devotions can evolve into a form of religious legalism devoid of genuine devotion, a habit lacking life and relationship. Devotion to God is a way of life, not simply a period of time reading Scripture or in prayer. Devotion to God must move from a specific practice to a daily being present with Him.

Consider the life of the Old Testament character Enoch. "When Enoch had lived 65 years, he became the father of Methuselah. After he became the father of Methuselah, Enoch walked faithfully with God 300 years and had other sons and daughters. Altogether, Enoch lived a total of 365 years. Enoch walked faithfully with God; then he was no more, because God took him away" (Genesis 5:21-24).

"By faith Enoch was taken from this life, so that he did not experience death: He could not be found, because God had taken him away. For before he was taken, he was commended as one who pleased God" (Hebrews 11:5). Enoch walked faithfully with God. Here is a picture of devotion. Such devotion pleased God.

Devotion to God is a pathway from self to the Sovereign. A God-devoted heart is a surrendered heart, an obedient heart, a God-pleasing heart. Daniel, the Israelite exile who became a high-ranking authority in Babylon, was known by his foreign peers as one who possessed such devotion. It was said of him that he set aside three specific times to face Jerusalem and pray. He worshipped only God, even under threat of death. Daniel's reputation was one of devotion to God.

We also see devotion beautifully expressed in Ruth's words to her mother-in-law Naomi. Naomi and Ruth both lost their husbands. Naomi pleads with Ruth to go to her own community where she will have a better opportunity for support and remarriage, but she replies, "Don't urge me to leave you or to turn back from you. Where you go I will go, and where you stay I will stay. Your people will be my people and your God my God. Where you die I will die, and there I will be buried. May the Lord deal with me, be it ever so severely, if even death separates you and me" (Ruth 1:16-17). Ruth committed her life to walking with Naomi. Above all Ruth wanted to be truly present with Naomi. I suggest that principles for devotion to God are captured in Ruth's words.

I found the connection between devotion and godliness an interesting one. New Testament Scripture is replete with counsel to pursue godliness (1 Timothy 4:8; Titus 2:11-13; 2 Peter 2:10-12). What is godliness? In his book, *The Practice Of Godliness*, Jerry Bridges writes that Godliness "... is devotion to God which results in a life that is pleasing to Him."[16] *Vines Expository Dictionary of Old and New Testament Words* defines godliness to be devout or to be devoted. Godliness is devotion.[17]

I believe that Enoch, Daniel and Ruth model for us

something significant: devotion. For Enoch and Daniel devotion was expressed by walking with God every day and living in a manner that pleased Him. Their names are in the hall of faith (Hebrews 11). Ruth modeled devotion through her commitment to Naomi. Today, thousands of years after Enoch, Daniel and Ruth walked the earth, we are still reading about the way they lived their lives. They exemplify for us genuine devotion.

Be blessed, my friends.

Letter Nine

REFLECTIONS

Letters to my Friends

LETTER TEN

Small, but Big

YOUR ATTITUDE DETERMINES YOUR ALTITUDE

"...whoever wants to be great among you must be your servant"
Matthew 20:26

"Not all of us can do great things.
But we can all do small things with great love."
Mother Teresa

Hello Friends.

Mother Teresa has often intrigued me. She was an Albanian Catholic nun who became a missionary; a small, seemingly fragile, woman who became world-renowned for her work amongst the poorest of the poor on the streets of Calcutta, India. For her labor, Mother Teresa received the Nobel Peace Prize. In her acceptance speech she began by thanking God and then said, "God loved the world so much that He sent His Son…Jesus Christ loved you and He loved me and gave His life for us…[Jesus] kept on saying: love as I have loved you…I am personally most unworthy… I am very happy to receive [this award] in the name of the hungry, of the naked, of the homeless, of the crippled, of the blind, of the leprous, of all those people who feel unwanted, unloved, uncared, thrown away of the society, people who have become a burden to the society, and are ashamed by everybody."[18] Today there are some one hundred charities operating in her name around the world; 4500 volunteers caring for the unloved. After her death, Mother Teresa was beatified. This diminutive woman became an official saint of the Catholic Church.

Mother Teresa was a genuine servant, the humblest of caregivers who changed her world and that of countless others. She lived amongst the poorest of the poor, but was welcomed by presidents, prime ministers, and kings. She stood only five feet tall but towered over others in her compassion and love for the sick and dying. She was small, but BIG!

We may not have known Mother Teresa, but we know

people who are like her – people with true servant's hearts, full of humility and selfless in spirit. They are not charismatic or colorful. They quietly give of themselves with no thought of recognition, no desire for attention, no ambition for being anything other than a help to others. These are the individuals most hardly notice, yet their influence is profound! When I look for role models to emulate, examples to follow, characteristics to mirror, I look to such as these; those who are small, but BIG.

There was One, born to peasant parents in a space that housed animals. This child started life in a feeding trough. There is almost no mention of this child's early years. He was not groomed by His parents for any grand career, just simple work as a tradesperson. At some thirty years of age He began to proclaim a message about God. He performed miraculous acts of healing the sick and those with disabilities, raising the dead and demonstrating power over nature. He taught with great wisdom and authority. Some called Him rabbi, others declared him a prophet, there were those who believed He was a king and a very small number wondered if they were not in the presence of the divine.

Repeatedly, He described Himself as a servant. He washed the feet of those He mentored. He said He did only what He was commanded to do by God. By His own testimony He claimed His life's purpose was to pour Himself out for others. He walked with the poor, the downtrodden, the marginalized, the sick, the broken, the demon possessed and the sinners. Eventually, He was arrested, tortured, and crucified. He died and was buried. A carpenter who loved the world so deeply that

He willingly laid down everything to save it.

Three days later He rose from the dead! He was like a small seed that is buried and then breaks forth from the ground to become a wondrous tree of life! This servant of the people, who gave His life for them, was revealed to be the very Son of God. The Bible says, "Christ Jesus: Who, being in very nature God, did not consider equality with God something to be used to his own advantage; rather, he made himself nothing by taking the very nature of a servant, being made in human likeness. And being found in appearance as a man, he humbled himself by becoming obedient to death—even death on a cross!" (Philippians 2:5b-8 NIV2). His sacrifice resulted in forgiveness of our sins, His resurrection our victory over death! Jesus was Mother Teresa's inspiration and more than that, her Lord and Savior. Jesus, the Prince of Peace, was the One to whom she pointed the world's leaders when she received the Nobel Peace award.

Consider the following statements made about Jesus:[19]

> "The character of Jesus has not only been the highest pattern of virtue, but the strongest incentive in its practice, and has exerted so deep an influence, that it may be truly said that the simple record of three years of active life has done more to regenerate and to soften mankind than all the disquisitions of philosophers and all the exhortations of moralists."
>
> W. E. H. Lecky, historian and political theorist
>
> "I know men and I tell you that Jesus Christ is no mere man.

Letter Ten

Between Him and every other person in the world there is no possible term of comparison. Alexander, Caesar, Charlemagne, and I have founded empires. But on what did we rest the creation of our genius? Upon force. Jesus Christ founded His empire upon love; and at this hour millions of men would die for Him."

Napoleon, military and political leader

"This Jesus of Nazareth, without money and arms, conquered more millions than Alexander, Caesar, Mohammed, and Napoleon; without science...he shed more light on things human and divine than all philosophers and scholars combined; without the eloquence of schools, he spoke such words of life as were never spoken before or since, and produced effects which lie beyond the reach of orator or poet; without writing a single line, he set more pens in motion, and furnished themes for more sermons, orations, discussions, learned volumes, works of art, and songs of praise than the whole army of great men of ancient and modern times."

Philip Schaff, theologian and historian

"I am an historian, I am not a believer, but I must confess as a historian that this penniless preacher from Nazareth is irrevocably the very center of history. Jesus Christ is easily the most dominant figure in all history."

H.G. Wells, historian and novelist

"As the centuries pass, the evidence is accumulating that, measured by His effect on history, Jesus is the most influential life ever lived on this planet."

Kenneth Scott Latourette, former president of the American Historical Association

He came to this world as a servant and left it as a savior. Jesus – small, but BIG. What is the message here for us? What are we to learn from Mother Teresa's example? What are we to learn from Jesus' example? What is here that will inform and transform our faith?

Be blessed, my friends.

Letter Ten

REFLECTIONS

Letters to my Friends

LETTER ELEVEN

Gripe or Grow

CHOOSING A PATH IN TROUBLED TIMES

"Our days may come to seventy years,
or eighty if our strength endures;
yet the best of them are but trouble and sorrow...."
Psalm 90:10

"Hardships often prepare ordinary people for
an extraordinary destiny."
C.S. Lewis

Hello Friends.

I am told from an unreliable source that listening to country music is the human cathartic channel in troubled times and that if you play these songs in reverse, you get your wife, dog and life back. My apologies to any offended real or poser cowboys or cowgirls riding about in steel mounts humming along to country tunes. Full disclosure, I find poking the country music 'bear' therapeutic. Seriously though, we live in troubled times. The devastating emotional and mental fallout alone is breathtaking. Moses, the great biblical patriarch, contends that trouble is a part of the human context and condition. Choosing a hopeful and helpful path in these and other troubled times seems glaringly intuitive for a disciple of Jesus.

As one who has trekked through times of trouble, I have gained some helpful perspective, maybe even wisdom. First, Moses was right that life is a journey of trouble. The school of life teaches us that from birth. Second, on this voyage across troubled waters God provides grace in many forms with the Gospel as the greatest example. Third, experiences of trouble always bring with them opportunities for blessing. Consider the lives of Moses, Joseph, Job and Paul to name a few. Finally, we have the freedom to gripe or grow in the face of these opportunities. Upon this last conviction I wish to humbly submit a few unpolished reflections.

In a previous letter I mentioned Viktor Emil Frankl's book, *Man's Search For Meaning* (1959). As a reminder, his work has sold more than ten million copies worldwide and is listed as one of the top ten most influential books in the United States. Frankl was a prisoner of the World War II concentration camps operated by the Nazi regime. Although his father, mother and wife perished, he survived. Frankl's experience was horrifying; profoundly inhuman. Out of his experiences Frankl wrote, *"We who lived in concentration camps can remember the men who walked through the huts comforting others, giving away their last piece of bread. They may have been few in number, but they offer sufficient proof that everything can be taken from a man but one thing: the last of the human freedoms – to choose one's attitude in any given set of circumstances, to choose one's own way."*[20] My sense is that most troubles come our way through forces beyond our control. How we respond to them, however, is not beyond our control. Gripe or grow. Your call.

The Italian Renaissance genius Leonardo da Vinci once said, "I love those who can smile in trouble." How many of these people are in your life? I know a handful and they are an inspiration. Their faces may not literally smile, but their countenance – their spirits – do. They possess a supernatural-like calmness in the storm. When trouble afflicts, they chose to grow, not gripe. These are disciples who translate their hardship into an opportunity to grow in faith. They choose to grow in humility and forbearance. They believe that troubles open a space where the Holy Spirit works to help them grow into Christlikeness. This conviction that troubles are a workshop of sorts for transformation causes me to pause and ponder upon the late author Terry Goodkind's claim: "If the road is easy, you're likely going the wrong way."[21]

Interestingly enough, my Anabaptist foreparents had a very similar conviction and even considered it a joy to endure troubles. Consider Swiss Anabaptist Conrad Grebel (1526) who wrote, "True Christian believers are sheep among wolves, sheep for the slaughter; they must be baptized in anguish and affliction, tribulation, persecution, suffering, and death; they must be tried with fire...."[22] Hendrick Alewijns (1569) and Jan Hendrikss (1571), two persecuted Anabaptists, connected their sufferings with the joy-in-trials spoken of in Scripture: "Dear brothers and sisters, when troubles of any kind come your way, consider it an opportunity for great joy" (James 1:2).

Granted, the examples I have given are at the extreme end on the scale of human troubles, however, they make a particularly strong case in that we do have the freedom to choose how we will respond, and that life's trials can provide an opportunity to grow, and even experience joy. Disciples of Christ who have lived through adversity and grown in their gentleness, humility and Christlikeness, inspire me. I am convinced that the true test of a healthy disciple is not how one behaves on their best days, but how one acts on the worst days. There is weight to the popular maxim "Adversity reveals character" and the wisdom of Helen Keller: "Character cannot be developed in ease and quiet. Only through experience of trial and suffering can the soul be strengthened, vision cleared, ambition inspired, and success achieved."[23]

And so, as our troubles and plights continue, my hope and prayer for us as disciples is that the troubles we encounter will reveal and foster godly character. May

Letter Eleven

your difficulties not translate into a space to gripe, but rather opportunities to grow into Christlikeness.

In this vein, I encourage you with these words of Scripture: "Let us fix our eyes on Jesus, the author and perfector of our faith, who for the joy set before him endured the cross..." (Hebrews 12:2a).

As a tip of my ten-gallon Stetson to country music-lovers, and in the spirit of these words I've penned, I recommend listening to Simon & Garfunkel's 1970 folk-rock tune *Bridge Over Troubled Water*. A 'salve' for the sorrowful cowboy (or cowgirl) soul.

Be blessed, my friends.

Letters to my Friends

REFLECTIONS

LETTER TWELVE

A Cat, a Tree, a Lesson

SOMETIMES THE BEST LESSONS ARE IN OUR BACKYARD

"To whom will you compare me? Or who is my equal?
Says the Holy One. Lift your eyes and look to the heavens...."
Isaiah 40:25-26a

"Begin each day with God. It will change your priorities."
Elizabeth George

Hello Friends.

Finnegan is our affectionate two-year-old tabby. Like all pets, Finnegan loves routines – things done repeatedly, in the same way. His expectation is simple and his pattern of behaviour varies little: bring a morning greeting chatter to Phil, receive a pat on the head and, enjoy a quick snack and then dash out the patio door into the back yard. As he gains his freedom (yes, he is tethered), Finnegan scampers across the lawn to our largest tree. At its base, he stops, rests on his hind quarters, and looks up. He remains in that posture for some time, quiet and looking up into the tree. Now, I know that he is predatory and likely hoping for an unaware chickadee to land too close. And, the rustling of the leaves fascinates him. But Finnegan's morning routine taught me something about my walk with the Lord.

The psalmist penned: "In the morning, O Lord, you hear my voice; in the morning I lay my requests before you and wait in expectation" (Psalm 5:3). I wondered if I was as faithful as Finnegan in making the start of every morning a time when I pause and look up (to my Heavenly Father), waiting in expectation. I think of Jesus: "Very early in the morning, while it was still dark, Jesus got up, left the house and went off to a solitary place, where he prayed" (Mark 1:35). He started His day by pausing life to look up. Scripture doesn't say whether this was an everyday practice for Jesus, but I like to think so.

I have found that when I start my day just dropping to my knees and looking up in expectation of my good Father's presence, I receive perspective, peace and strength. I am given the words of Isaiah 41:10: "So do not fear, for I am with you; do not be dismayed, for I am your God. I will strengthen you and help you with my righteous right hand." Indeed, God's compassions, His mercies and loving-kindness are new every morning (Lamentations 3:23).

Finnegan, thanks for reminding me every morning to pause life and consider my routine. I sense you are blessed by what you discover in the tree. I know I am both blessed and prompted to look up when I watch you.

Be blessed, my friends.

REFLECTIONS

LETTER THIRTEEN

There Once was a Man

SEEING PAST OUR TROUBLES

"Because of the Lord's great love we are not consumed,
for his compassions never fail. They are new every morning;
great is your faithfulness."
Lamentations 3:22-23

"Great faith must endure great trials."
L.B. Cowman

Letters to my Friends

Hello Friends.

There are times in life when troubles seem to bubble up all around us, and difficulties of various kinds threaten to overwhelm us. At times like these – pandemic times, that is – I find comfort and wisdom in Job's response to his circumstances. After the loss of his wealth and family, Job grieves and then worships: "...may the name of the LORD be praised" (1:20-21). After the loss of his health Job acknowledges God's sovereignty: "Shall we accept good from God and not trouble" (2:10). In both situations Job "...did not sin by charging God with wrong-doing" (1:22; 2:10). Later, as he wrestles with the counsel of his wife and friends he declares, "Though [the LORD] slay me, yet will I hope in him..." (13:15). Despite his new normal, the LORD remains his anchor, his truth and his trust. Embedded in Job's claim is the conviction that, although at times a mystery, God and His ways are righteous.

The story continues. Job declares, "I know that my Redeemer lives..." (19:25). Job's belief is that there is one who will turn his circumstances around; one who will relieve his suffering and restore and rebuild his life. After God has revealed himself through a series of claims about his place as the world's Creator and Sustainor, Job acknowledges: "My ears have heard of you but now my eyes have seen you" (42:5). His eyes have been opened to a much deeper understanding of who it is he trusts and worships. No doubt, his worship of the LORD is on a whole new and life-transforming plateau.

How shall we then live? The story of Job has much wisdom to offer us, but perhaps the most profound truth is that when our faith is anchored to a Sovereign God, there is hope, redemption and transformation in all things. Job's story ends with a new family, a new wealth, a new wellness and a life that is "full of years" (42:17). To have lived a life "full of years" is understood as one rich in the grace and blessing of God.

This bumpy life we live continues unfettered by our wishes, wants or worries. It has been, is or will be difficult; such is the state of our fallen world. I call you to consider Job, his life, his story and his response to the 'new normal' he faced. May you be strengthened, encouraged and drawn to worship Him who "laid the earth's foundation" and "brought forth the constellations" (38:4,32).

Be blessed, my friends.

Letters to my Friends

REFLECTIONS

LETTER FOURTEEN

Sabbath

Letters to my Friends

Hello Friends.

American writer John Updike wrote, "Rain is grace; rain is the sky condescending to the earth; without rain, there would be no life." Updike's words and Todd Agnew's song "Grace Like Rain" spoke into my life as I was writing my own version of *"Grace Like Rain"* on January 1, 2012, in Regina, Saskatchewan.

GRACE LIKE RAIN

Grace like rain falls down on me,
    a blessing without fail.
It wakes me up, stands me straight,
    and sets my life a-sail.
It springs from depths of love divine,
    a heart so wholly pure.
It knows no bounds nor fears no risk,
    in all things is a cure.
It spreads before me daily bread,
    meets every need with care.
It goes beyond the things I know,
    responds to every prayer.
It opens doors to untouched shores,
    it sets my spirit free.
It wipes my slate completely clean,
    no sin to impede me.
It makes aright my inner soul,
    gives peace in every gale.
All devils, curses, evils dark,
    cannot 'gainst grace prevail.

Letter Fourteen

It is by grace that I am saved,
    reborn, redeemed, no blame.
Grace like rain falls down on me,
    let it rain, let it rain, let it rain.*

**Heartwork – II Grace Like Rain*, PG, 2012.

SABBATH PRAYER

Morning Prayer was written in 1999 and included in a morning worship service at Parliament Community Church (Regina, Saskatchewan) on April 17, 1999. It was revised in 2011. It was penned as an expression of praise and worship during my first year as pastor of the church.

> "In the morning, my prayer comes before you."
> Psalm 88:13

> "It is not so true that prayer changes things as that
> prayer changes me and I change things."
> Oswald Chambers

MORNING PRAYER

Rock of ages, our great King and Shepherd, accept us into Your
    presence this morning.
Father of all things good and pure, it is our desire to be pleasing
    in Your sight.
We come not in our own righteousness, but in the name of Jesus
    Your Son.
With hearts raised in worship, we acknowledge that in You, and
    You alone, we live
    and move and have our being.
May our meditations and songs be a pure offering.
May our thoughts feast on the bread of heaven and not the dust
    of the earth.
May our fellowship permeate with sweet gentleness and
    encouragement and

Letter Fourteen

not with the foul ill-will.
May our minds be like dry sponges seeking the moisture of
 living water.
Father of all compassion, anoint the hearts of those here this
 morning who are
  burdened and whose very souls are brimming with the
  tears of uncertainty, pain, illness, depression, conflict, or
  loneliness.
Restore unto them this morning the joy of Your Spirit.
Fill with gladness those whose cup overflows with celebration.
Bring assurance to those who doubt, faith to those who question
 and to all of us, bring a
 sense of Your divine presence.
We raise up to you the Christians suffering devastation this day.
Pour forth the power of Your Spirit into their hearts so that they
 may voice Your saving
 name to all who have ears.
Pour forth also the oil of Your compassion upon these brothers
 and sisters so that they
 might be that cup of cold water to others.
We pray for worldwide revival and praise You for such a reality
 already taking place in
 so many areas around the globe. Bring forth revival we pray.
We pray for the conflict within our own province and invite Your
 Spirit to mould, shape,
 direct and comfort the believers on both sides of all issues.
 We lift up the sick, both young and old, who fear for
 their care.
We pray for the removal of pride and the outpouring of empathy.
We pray for our government, for wisdom and discernment
 Accept our offering as a token of our desire to

    expand Your
        Kingdom on earth.
May we offer it with joy and not a spirit of duty.
Hear us O Shepherd of Israel.
Make Your grace issue forth from heaven's glorious domain.
May we experience a shower of joy in our worship of Your
    high and Holy name.
For You, and You alone, are the true Great One.
We pray this in Jesus' name, with Thanksgiving. Amen*

*Heartwork – An Endless Hallelujah, PG, 2011

Letter Fourteen

REFLECTIONS

WEEK III

LETTER FIFTEEN

Hurry Up and Slow Down

**THINKING DIFFERENTLY ABOUT
RUSH AND HASTE**

"Be still...."
Psalm 46:10a

"God did not create hurry."
Finnish Proverb

Hello Friends.

By nature or nurture I seem to be predisposed to live a rushed life, to touch the red zone of overload, to speed through tasks, experiences, conversations and sadly, I often try to rush spiritual formation as well. In 2011, at the starting line of my first ever sabbatical, I completely ruptured my Achilles tendon playing basketball with high school friends. All of my plans for my sabbatical, including my travel to Israel, Turkey and Egypt, and the adventures in the mountains of Vancouver Island, came to an abrupt end. I spent 16 weeks in a cast and months in rehab. I was forced to rest and cease striving. After I worked through some significant frustration and disappointment, the Lord had my attention. As I recovered from my injury, I was able to encounter the Lord in fresh ways. I heard His voice and experienced His love, joy and peace in life-transforming ways. Two of the most profound faith lessons I learned were that all things I experienced had a purpose and that healthy spiritual formation came when I was both still and available to the Lord. My forced rest brought profound blessing.

Christian author Richard A. Swenson wrote, "Very little of lasting spiritual value happens in the presence of speed."[24] Eugene Peterson said, "Busyness is the enemy of spirituality."[25] Friends, I encourage you as Christocentric people to consider Jesus' life. There were countless demands on His time, but was He ever in a hurry? There were urgent matters Jesus dealt with, but was He ever rushed? His life was full from morning until evening, but would you describe Jesus as living without margins or lacking a measured pace? His was a life of purpose not haste.

There is much for us to learn here as Jesus' followers. Sadly, as Christians we often understand being on fire for Jesus as burning out for Him – we burn the candle at both ends and expect God to honour such a practice. The number of Christian leaders failing in ministry due to lack of life margins, suffering panic attacks or becoming burnt out and requiring medication is growing exponentially. In addition, Christians are often guilty of not practicing healthy forms of sabbath. Again, Swenson writes, "If God were our appointment secretary, would He schedule us for every minute of every day?"[26]

Christian author Roy Lessin once said, "There is always time enough in a day to do God's will."[27] There is wisdom in Lessin's claim. The Lord indeed has ordained our days (Psalm 139), but he does not require a life of rushing to and fro, speeding from one task to the next, overloaded and overwhelmed. "Be still (cease striving) and know that I am God" (Psalm 46:10) should be woven into the fabric of our lives as Christians. Perhaps we would then have fewer emotional and mental injuries amongst our ranks.

The 2020 – 2022 pandemic provided me with another opportunity to cease striving. I had no appointments other than virtual ones, less administrative work as most events were postponed and less travel by car or plane as government restrictions all but halted such opportunities. Haste and hurry are casualties in my life. The pandemic reminded me once again that God is sovereign (all things we experience have a purpose) and that healthy spiritual formation comes as we are still and available.

Be blessed, my friends.

Letter Fifteen

REFLECTIONS

Letters to my Friends

LETTER SIXTEEN

Hurry Sickness, My Fresh Insight

MAKING TIME AND SPACE FOR THINGS THAT MATTER MOST

"Wait for the Lord; be strong and take
heart and wait for the Lord."
Psalm 27:14

"Haste has no blessings."
Swahili proverb

Hello Friends.

During my vacation, I consumed John Mark Comer's book, *The Ruthless Elimination of Hurry*. I read through most of it in one sitting; the message resonated with me in a deep and profound way. As disciples, I recommend you place this work on your priority reading list. Caution, it may transform your life!

There is far too much wisdom in this book for me to possibly squeeze into a piece like this, however, I will share an aspect of the book that gave me a fresh leadership insight. This arresting cognizance concerned the relationship between time and love.

Any love relationship requires a significant investment of our time. This is true of the love relationship between a husband and wife, a parent and child, and as Christians, between us and Jesus. We speak of walking, abiding, resting and being still with Jesus. Abiding time is simply a key ingredient. This is inherent in love relationships. Consider Scripture's *Love Chapter* (1 Corinthians 13). When the Apostle Paul put pen to parchment describing what love was, his first descriptor was that love was *"patient"* – in other words, *give it time*.

The challenge for disciples today is that we battle *"Hurry Sickness."* First coined by Dr. Fred Meyer in the 1950s, Hurry Sickness is characterized by an unrelenting desire to achieve more in less time.[28] And so, we super-multitask, work a ton of overtime and acquire whatever technology needed to increase our efficiency. The problem is that *"hurry and love are incompatible,"* writes Comer.[29] He makes a further claim that peace and joy are also incompatible with hurry.

Simply put, hurry – living in a rush – makes us sick. Countless scientific surveys have proven this reality.

Comer provides a list of Hurry Sickness symptoms including (in part) irritability, hypersensitivity, restlessness, workaholism, and escapist behaviors. However, the most poignant symptom for disciples is the deterioration of our love relationship with God. Disciples could end up doing wonderful religious things for the God who is absent from our lives. Hurry risks our love relationship with Jesus. Comer states, "Love takes time; hurry doesn't have it." Christian author John Ortberg writes, "I cannot live in the Kingdom of God with a hurried soul."[30] These are sobering words which call for careful reflection by disciples in a hypersonic-paced culture. In our world of rush and hurry, consider in a new way the words of Jesus: "Come to me, all you who are weary and burdened, and I will give you rest" (Matthew 11:28).

If you value your love relationship with Jesus, take Hurry Sickness seriously. Rediscover what Dr. Peter Scazzero calls a *slowdown spirituality*.[31]

Be blessed, my friends.

Letters to my Friends

REFLECTIONS

LETTER SEVENTEEN

Life Editing – Life Decluttering

THE POWER OF LETTING GO

"To everything there is a season, and a time to every purpose under the heaven...a time to keep and a time to cast away."
Ecclesiastes 3:1,6b KJV

"The secret of happiness, you see, is not found in seeking more, but in developing the capacity to enjoy less."
Socrates

Hello Friends.

As a senior pastor I made it a practice to engage in annual refocusing sessions with each member of the church staff. Invariably, when asked how they were managing their specific ministry responsibilities, the response would be something like, *"I'm struggling to get my work done."* All staff completed time logs which helped me pinpoint potential problem areas. In most cases the staff member's sense of being overwhelmed boiled down to a failure to focus on key ministry roles and responsibilities. As a result, ministry drift took place.

Instead of accomplishing the core tasks of their ministry, staff added non-essential activities to their schedule. These may have been good things, but doing them undermined effectiveness, efficiency, and in several cases, pushed them beyond their capacity to maintain a healthy ministry. In order to bring back a sense of well-being and balance, I asked staff to do some ministry-editing and decluttering: *What is essential to your role/calling? What have you added that is non-essential? What needs to happen for you to get back to effectiveness, balance and margin?*

Cluttering one's life with non-essentials and joy-draining distractions goes well beyond vocational ministry. I would venture to say that a large number of disciples have very-little-to-no margin in their life, certainly a fragile overall life balance. Too many disciples live a life of rush, red-lining stress, and a despairing sense they are failing to keep up *(picture a pudgy hamster on his wheel here)*. I am completely convinced that no healthy life, spiritual formation or ministry, happens in a rush. Living life under constant stress reaps things like ulcers and cardio-vascular ailments. And, living under the cloud of feeling like you simply aren't keeping up breeds anxiety, despair and eventually depression. If I'm describing you, a trip to your physician or therapist is a wise move. After that, consider some life-editing and decluttering.

Life-editing and decluttering is about assessing how you are journeying your finite, God-given time on earth and then, addressing any aspects which keep you from being in a space of balance and margin. A wise person once told me that everything you pick up you can let go; everything you get encumbered with you can separate from. A practice adopted can be released. And, a habit formed can be transformed. Great counsel. Over time I have learned to know that there is freedom in letting things go, especially those things that rob one of joy, peace and purpose. What is it that you need to let go? Seriously, what in your life is devouring your precious non-renewable time and leaving you feeling like you just drank a tumbler of vinegar?

American philosopher and poet Henry David Thoreau made popular his declaration, live deliberately.[32] This is thoughtful counsel. On another plain, the Holy Spirit routinely nudges me to soak in these words of the psalmist: "Lord, remind me how brief my time on earth will be. Remind me that my days are numbered— how fleeting my life is. You have made my life no longer than the width of my hand. My entire lifetime is just a moment to you; at best, each of us is but a breath" (Psalm 39:4-5). Knowing that your life is like the fleeting morning mist, how urgent is Spirit-led life-editing and life-decluttering? It's your one life; you decide.

> "Teach us to number our days aright, that we may gain a heart of wisdom."
> Psalm 90:12

Be blessed, my friends.

Letter Seventeen

REFLECTIONS

Letters to my Friends

LETTER EIGHTEEN

My Battle with 'Vertigo'

MARGINS AND LIFE BALANCE

"But they that wait upon the Lord shall renew their strength."
Isaiah 40:31a TLB

"Whatever else it may be, life is one big balancing act."
Sherwin B. Nuland, MD

Hello Friends.

Benign paroxysmal positional vertigo, the physical sensation of extreme dizziness, has been my thorn-in-the-side for five years. One spell of just seconds can render me feeling nauseous and off-balance for hours. It is not uncommon for me to have one a day. When I experience an episode, I will do most anything to regain immediate balance. I have adjusted my lifestyle to compensate for this chronic condition. I engage my ailment with utmost seriousness. I limit my activities to those that require very little movement (no amusement park rides for me) and avoid head positions that trigger episodes (no more handstands). Daily, I appeal to God for healing. I also pray for grace as I wait. I remind myself that there is purpose in this struggle.

I also battle with balance of another kind – life balance. Equalizing my time in abiding with Jesus, caring for myself and my family's well-being, and fulfilling my ministry responsibilities, is a formidable task. I know I am not alone in this tug-of-war over time and priorities. I have experienced at least one period in my life when I came face-to-face with burnout. Using a tachometer metaphor, my capacity to effectively engage life was in the 'red.' I responded by making significant changes to how I viewed my emotional and spiritual capacity, said 'no' to most asks on my time, and participated in life-giving pursuits such as listening prayer, exercise and pursuing activities that brought me joy and rest. Today I am well aware of my personal capacity, I guard my margins and I am sensitive to what my well-being 'gauges' are telling me.

Jesus exemplified a balanced life. He prioritized time with the Father, maintained a healthy well-being (including personal relationships) and engaged successfully in ministry priorities such as caring for people, mentoring the disciples, preaching and teaching. He literally had the cosmic weight of humanity on his shoulders, and yet he lived a peace and balance beyond understanding. I continue to be inspired by Jesus as I wrestle with my own life balance orientation. Like a gyroscope, Jesus' example helps me achieve stability and direction in this life. Jesus is my life stabilizer; my proverbial equalizer so-to-speak.

In the book *In Search of Balance* Richard A. Swenson writes, "Our difficulty in recovering balance and then sustaining what we have recovered is that balance is not a single-point-source problem. Everywhere we look, we see the battle lines."[33] The challenge of maintaining a healthy life balance is a great one and many have fallen to defeat, some never to recover. That being said, there is hope. I have experienced victories in my own struggle and learned much. I encourage you to persevere, but you must act proactively and sooner rather than later. You play a role in this battle to conquer life balance vertigo. The following are my helps as I walk the pathway to a balanced life:

- Own the problem. Personal accountability is ground zero for building a balanced life. Admit personal limits and understand that exceeding them will result in disorientation.

- Seek the counsel of the Holy Spirit and other wise advisors. This practice is needed in order to accomplish the deep soul work around how and why one is spending their life as they do. Too often we wear blinders. We need the discernment of others.
- Assess the expectations you and others have on your most limited resource, time. What is and isn't realistic and healthy? Unmet expectations rapidly rob us of joy.
- Examine your history of investing time. What needs to stop, continue, be somewhat changed? Is there anything that needs to begin?
- Ask yourself, am I doing enough that is truly life-giving? Am I engaging in activities to promote physical health (regular exercise, sufficient rest, balanced diet)? Am I guarding my margins? I once owned a sports car, and I was always careful to keep the vehicle's rpms out of the 'red' otherwise the engine was in danger of a malfunction. In our own contexts, without personal time boundaries, we malfunction as disciples, we become unable serve Jesus and others and instead need help ourselves.
- Ponder whether or not you are truly cherishing the right things. For me, this is abiding with the Lord, spending time with family and friends, and pouring into my passions.

May these helps assist you to avoid, or come to terms with, life balance vertigo.

There is an Irish proverb that says, "When God created time, he made plenty of it." However, so many of us have stumbled by not choosing the right things into which to pour our time or perhaps being unable to correctly apply

Letter Eighteen

the appropriate amount of time we invest in activities. Johann Wolfgang von Goethe counseled, "Things that matter most, must never be at the mercy of things that matter least."[34]

Be blessed, my friends.

Letters to my Friends

REFLECTIONS

LETTER NINETEEN

Dad's Secret of Contentment

RESTING IN THE SOVEREIGNTY OF GOD

"I have learned the secret of contentment in every situation."
Philippians 4:12

"My Father always knows what is best."
Peter Wall Gunther

Hello Friends.

During my dad's home stretch to heaven, I had memorable dialogues with him about his life journey. He was born in southern Russia during the turbulent 1930's, grew up under the dictatorial rule of Stalin, experienced the horrors of WWII, saw his father arrested and eventually imprisoned in a Siberian work camp, helped his mother and siblings flee from communist persecution across the vast wasteland of post-war Europe, and settled on a rural Manitoba homestead, enduring the harsh realities of a prairie winter. He owned nothing other than what he was wearing at the time. He lost a sister on the exodus. Such experiences left many of his generation with deep psychological scars, a spirit of bitterness, and despair. Dad, however, spoke of being content as he started a new life in Canada – "We didn't have much," he'd say, "but we had each other, and the Lord." His new life in Canada included back-breaking work, living with the bare necessities, raising six children, moving the family across Canada to start a new business, and being the recipient of both goodwill and malice. In the latter part of his life, he lost health, mobility, clarity of thought, parents, siblings, close friends, a son, and his wife. What is remarkable to me is although each of these came with initial pangs of grief and pain, it was not long before he began expressing his sense of contentment with life. Let me be clear, my dad had struggles, made mistakes, had worries, and battled moments of anxiety. However, he would always return to a sense of what I call a contentment equilibrium, anchored to Christ. "My life is not about me, but about Him whom I serve. Christ is first," was his mantra.

I never specifically asked my dad why he could always return to a space of contentment, but it was genuinely present. I saw it even later in his life when he experienced serious health issues followed by a cascade of downsizing from a large farm to a retirement condo, to a small room in an assisted living complex (a sterile abode with a few trinkets from eighty plus years of life). After the death of my younger brother and mother, he still returned to a sense of quiet contentment before too long. Yes, there were definitely moments of mourning and loneliness, but these seemed temporary. He was like a human version of memory foam, which, after being crushed by a weight, soon returns back to form. After pondering our last conversations, I began to sense the secret of dad's contentment.

When talking about his life's narrative, especially the painful stretches, he would say, "Philip, our Father always knows what is best; he makes no mistakes." He would routinely suggest that when facing hardship, I should not ask God to remove its weight, but rather ask him for a stronger 'back' to carry it. After the deaths of my youngest brother and mother he wondered why he was left behind and then concluded, "My Father has something more for me in this life, I will listen for his voice and encourage others." Dad lived to encourage, especially those he felt were grieving or bitter. Dad lived by the maxim "Be somebody who makes everybody feel like a somebody." I surmise that dad's gift of being an encourager sprung, in part, from his unflappable sense of contentment.

"Contentment is an extension of trust," penned Richard A. Swenson.[35] There are two realities at play in every person's life; the earthly temporal and the heavenly eternal. We live in the first as created beings with finite understanding and perspective. God is not so limited. A maxim I grew up with is that God knows the end from the beginning (Isaiah 46:10). It simply means that God is omnipotent, omniscient and omnipresent. Contentment is trusting that God is indeed all these things even if everything we are presently experiencing in our temporal reality says otherwise. Thomas Jacomb, a 17th century English minister, stated, "Contentment imports calmness and composedness of mind in every condition- stillness and sedateness of spirit under all occurrences of providence. When a man likes whatsoever God doeth to him or with him...this is contentment."[36]

Etched into my dad's heart were the sentiments of Paul's counsel to the church in Rome, "And we know that God causes everything to work together for the good of those who love God and are called according to his purpose for them" (Romans 8:28). The apostle's conviction (and my dad's) around contentment were embedded in a personal understanding and experience of the love, grace and sovereignty of God (Philippians 4:12). Dad's secret of contentment was perhaps less complex than many believe. As he saw it, it was living from a place of (using a common expression) letting go and letting God, because the Father does indeed know what is best.

Be blessed, my friends.

Letter Nineteen

REFLECTIONS

Letters to my Friends

LETTER TWENTY

Contentment: The Path Less Travelled

IT'S ABOUT WHOSE YOU ARE

"A humble, reverent walk with God leads to life,
then one rests content, not shaken in times of trouble."
Proverbs 19:23

"Discontent is the joy of the devils."
Thomas Watson

Hello Friends.

Full disclosure, I have times when I do not experience contentment. I demonstrate moments of discontent. However, I do eventually land in a space I call contentment equilibrium. Like you, I am on a journey to a spiritual satisfaction in Christ. The following is what I have learned about contentment. It has enabled me to better walk this journey.

> "Contentment is a deep emotional state of being where a mysterious mixture of acceptance, hope, satisfaction, gratitude, peace and joy abide."
> *Pilgrimage Journals* [37]

I recently re-discovered Barry Adams' 1999 work, *The Father's Love Letter*.[38] Translated into over 100 languages this literary piece is a compilation of verses from the Bible to form a single epistle from God. Adams, formerly an associate pastor in a Mennonite church in St. Catharines, Ontario, intended that each line in the letter be paraphrased to communicate the depth and breadth of God's love for humankind. At the same time, I was reading Richard Swensen's book, *Contentment – The Secret to a Lasting Calm*, and Thomas Watson's work, *The Art of Divine Contentment*. All of these sources expanded my horizons on the nature of contentment. I particularly engaged with Watson's assertions. This 17th century English Puritan pastor taught that contentment springs from understanding God's providential care and from trusting in the very promises of God. Watson wrote,

> "He has taken you out of the wild olive vine of nature, and grafted you into Christ, making you living branches of that living vine. He has not only caused the light to shine on you, but into you, and has granted you all the privileges of sonship. Is not here that which may make the soul content?"[39]

Adams makes a truly inspiring effort to edify and encourage disciples of Jesus. He counsels that God sees you and me as the beloved. He outlines in point form the spectrum of God's loving and redemptive work on our behalf. Watson posits that it is these salvific expressions and promises of God that are the basis of contentment. Freedom in Christ ministry founder Neil Anderson's work on equipping disciples has a place here. Anderson wants to help believers experience freedom and vitality in life based upon understanding their identity in Christ. It is when they accept and live out of who they are in Christ that they will experience contentment.

In my exploration, I too gravitate to the notion that my own personal contentment is deeply rooted in the nature, work and promises of God. In my journal I drafted ten contentment circuit breakers (see article inset). A circuit breaker is a device which interrupts the flow of electricity stopping the function of some electronic component. Similarly, there are contentment circuit breakers. They interrupt our connection to a deep and life-giving walk with God, and as a result contentment is lost. What I noticed is that most of them seem to circle around a shallow understanding of God – what he has done, is doing and will do in our lives, not accepting our God-given identity in Christ, or doubting God's promises.

TEN CONTENTMENT CIRCUIT BREAKERS

1. Lack of faith in God's sovereignty
2. Doubting the goodness of God, and his love
3. Eyes fixed on something other than Jesus
4. Lack of gratitude, not seeing one's blessings
5. A mind fixed on earthly matters
6. Covetousness
7. Misunderstanding the purpose of hardship and suffering
8. Soaking in social media rather than sacred Scripture
9. Failure to understand, accept and live out of one's identity in Christ
10. Unconfessed sin

In pastoral ministry I witnessed many discontented Christians – too many, in fact. When I reflect on the possible reasons for so many casualties to this unsettling emotional state, one or more of the circuit-breakers come to mind. Watson crafted a unique perspective here when he wrote to his 17th century audience, "The discontented person thinks everything he does for God is too much, and everything that God does for him is too little."[40] I would simply add, far too many disciples are discontent because they don't genuinely know or accept the path our kind Father has laid before them, a road paved with the knowledge that he will treat his disciples as his beloved. Swenson wisely pens, "We will only be whole – at peace, at rest, and fully contented – when we agree with God about who we are and about what He wants us to be."[41]

I have come to accept that contentment exists as a learned

reality. The Apostle Paul wrote to the church in Philippi, "I have learned the secret of being content in any and every situation" (Philippians 4:12b). Contentment is also a choice we make, a biblical command we are to obey, actually (1 Timothy 6:8; Hebrews 13:5). Finally, contentment is a work of the Holy Spirit (Galatians 5:22-25). Author Jeremiah Burroughs, in his book, *The Rare Jewel of Christian Contentment* wrote that, "Contentment is a sweet, inward heart thing. It is the work of the Spirit indoors."[42]

American poet Robert Frost wrote a poem called *The Road Not Taken* in which he described two roads that lay before him in the yellow wood; one was well worn, the other "less traveled by."[43] He took the latter and that made all the difference. I tend to think about contentment in a similar way; the paths of discontent and contentment are stretched out before us. The latter road is sadly less traveled by, even for disciples, but choosing it makes all the difference.

Be blessed, my friends.

Letters to my Friends

REFLECTIONS
___

LETTER TWENTY-ONE

Sabbath

Hello Friends.

"Be still and know that I am God; I will be exalted among the nations, I will be exalted in the earth" (Psalm 46:10). Mother Teresa said, "I always begin my prayer in silence, for it is in the silence of the heart that God speaks." In his book, *Spiritual Disciplines For The Christian Life*, Donald S. Whitney writes, "Without silence and solitude we're shallow." In my own spiritual formation, I have never fostered faith and conviction more than when I spent time with God in solitude and silence. *The Sacred Stillness* was first penned on October 17, 2012 in Regina, Saskatchewan.

THE SACRED STILLNESS

>The Lord is not in the clatter
>>the buzz
>>the racket
>
>Cease your striving
>>your rush
>>your noise
>
>Hush the disquiet of your heart
>>the babble of your mind
>>the din of your soul
>
>God abides in the sacred stillness.
>
>He inhabits the lull
>>the calm
>>the peace

Letter Twenty-One

He is in the silence
        the interlude
        the quiet

God waits for you in the sacred stillness.

SABBATH PRAYER

The Lord's brother James instructed the believers of the ancient church, sometime around 48 A.D.: "If any of you lacks wisdom, he should ask God, who gives generously to all without finding fault, and it will be given to him" (James 1:5). James also described a wisdom not from this earth, but from heaven, a wisdom that is, "…pure; then peace-loving, considerate, submissive, full of mercy and good fruit, impartial and sincere" (James 3:17). *Prayer For Wisdom* was put to paper on January 22, 2012, in Los Cabos, Mexico.

> "But if you lack wisdom, you should pray to God, who will give it to you; because God gives generously and graciously to all."
> James 1:5 GNT

> "Prayer is aligning ourselves with the purposes of God."
> E. Stanley Jones

PRAYER FOR WISDOM

God, I seek wisdom, heavenly wisdom,
> wisdom that comes from your heart.

Grant me wisdom to discern truth from
> error, good from evil.

Bless me with the wisdom to understand and
> obey your ways.

Fill me with the kind of wisdom I need to love
> you with all my heart and others as
> myself.

Letter Twenty-One

Pour out upon me the wisdom to live
    passionately, serve with humility,
    and speak with integrity.
Give me the wisdom needed to make decisions
    that build up rather than tear down,
    encourage rather than condemn.
Lord, I search for wisdom that inspires others
    to live lives pleasing to you.
Gift me with wisdom to know hope in
    hardship, joy in suffering, and peace in
    the turmoil of trials.
Bless me with the wisdom to be both a skilled
    and gracious steward of my time and
    resources.
Grant me the wisdom to choose the right path
    to journey amongst all the noble ones.
May I truly love your wisdom more than the
    treasures of the earth.
May it set a garland of grace upon me.
I pray in expectation with thanksgiving.
Amen.

REFLECTIONS

Letter Twenty-One

WEEK IV

Letters to my Friends

LETTER TWENTY-TWO

Bold Benevolence

IT IS AMAZING WHAT KINDNESS CAN DO

"Go and do likewise."
Jesus, The Good Samaritan, Luke 10:37

"Treat people with kindness, because behind every face is a
story that could use a little more love."
Cheryl Richardson

Hello Friends.

This week I soaked in the inspiring words of Quaker William Penn: "I expect to pass through life but once. If therefore, there be any kindness I can show, or any good thing I can do to any fellow being, let me do it now, and not defer or neglect it, as I shall not pass this way again."

The Father is affording us many unique opportunities for bold benevolence – the quality of being courageously well meaning. During the pandemic season for example, the fear and despair of many individuals presented multiple occasions for disciples of Jesus to do good. It was during this time period when I came across a handwritten sign taped onto the front window of a Starbucks: *"Today you could be standing next to someone who is trying their best not to fall apart. Whatever you do today, do it with kindness in your heart."* Then there was this plastic sandwich board on Kelowna's downtown waterfront promenade which messaged: *"Spread kindness, not germs."* Friends, as disciples what more encouragement do we need?

Biblically, we see bold benevolence in the Good Samaritan narrative. Here Jesus explodes our limitations on those to whom we are to be kind. Strangers, even enemies, are to be the recipients of our love and blessing. In the world's time of darkness the call of Jesus is striking: "…let your light shine before others, that they may see your good deeds and glorify your Father in heaven" (Matthew 6:16).

Consider the striking maxim: *A life not lived for others is not a life.* I wonder if Jesus used these same words when he journeyed this earth. Aside from Jesus, Mother

Teresa epitomizes for me a person who was profoundly other-centered. I am certainly not Mother Teresa nor am I suggesting you be. However, I am asking, are acts of bold benevolence a daily part of my life?

Concerning bold benevolence, a wise person counselled me that a disciple of Jesus must pray for a supernatural transformation of one's heart. Why? Because our default is to be self-centered. The Holy Spirit's help is needed in order for us to be genuinely other-centered. Consider Menno Simon's definition of true evangelical faith; it aligns with this bold benevolence:

"For true evangelical faith is of such a nature that it cannot lay dormant;
but manifests itself in all righteousness and works of love;
it dies unto flesh and blood;
destroys all forbidden lusts and desires;
cordially seeks, serves and fears God;
clothes the naked; feeds the hungry;
consoles the afflicted; shelters the miserable;
aids and consoles all the oppressed;
returns good for evil;
serves those that injure it;
prays for those that persecute it;
teaches, admonishes and reproves with the Word of the Lord;
seeks that which is lost; binds up that which is wounded;
heals that which is diseased and saves that which is sound.
The persecution, suffering and anxiety which befalls it for the sake of the truth of the Lord,
is to it a glorious joy and consolation."[45]

With Simon's sentiments in mind, I also must ask if I am even *available* to be a good Smartian in another's life? Does my life have margin for deliberate genuine acts of kindness?

As I write this piece, I can't help humming the 1909 hymn *Make Me a Blessing* written by Ira B. Wilson. Here is a part of his memorable work:

"Out in the highways and byways of life, Many are weary and sad; Carry the sunshine where darkness is rife, Making the sorrowing glad.

Make me a blessing, make me a blessing, Out of my life may Jesus shine; Make me a blessing, O Savior, I pray. Make me a blessing to someone today."

Friends, during times of uncertainty, anxiety, and fear, be the reason someone smiles. I think Jesus will approve.

Be blessed, my friends.

Letter Twenty-Two

REFLECTIONS

Letters to my Friends

LETTER TWENTY-THREE

Another's Troubles

PERFORMING 'HAPPY DANCES' WHEN OTHERS FALL IS A DISCIPLESHIP FAIL

"As God's chosen people, holy and dearly loved,
clothe yourselves with...kindness."
Colossians 3:12

"It is in your hands to create a better world for all who live in it."
Nelson Mandela

Hello Friends.

Rarely have I found the sentiments of Hollywood actors of substance. I must say, however, the words of the late comedian Robin Williams have merit: "Everyone you meet is fighting a battle you know nothing about. Be kind. Always."[46]

"Be kind. Always." This seems so basic to being a disciple of Jesus (Luke 6:31). Realistically, it seems doable when it involves people we like. When it involves the antagonists in our life, that's a whole other matter, right? In Christ we love others, but in our flesh, we don't necessarily like all those others. In general, I do not believe I am intentionally malicious toward the difficult people in my life, but the truth is when they fall, sometimes I inwardly relish it. Another's trouble sometimes has me tempted to perform the proverbial happy dance. Just trying to be real here. Is this resonating with you?

Of course, this does not apply to your favourite sports team crushing their competitors or that terrible political party being voted out of office...just sayin'. It does apply to those who disagree with us about our leadership style, don't support us in our work or those who have hurt us by their actions.

Scripture has some counsel here: "Do not gloat when your enemy fails; when they stumble, do not let your hearts rejoice" (Proverbs 24:17). "You should not gloat over your brother in the day of his misfortune..." (Obadiah 1:12). To gloat is to relish with malignant pleasure the misfortune of another. "In your hearts do not

Letter Twenty-Three

think evil of each other" (1 Corinthians 16:14).

What we think about others shapes the way we treat them. This is a relationship 101 principle. Gloating at the misfortunes of another seems like a discipleship fail. It certainly isn't listed among the *one-anothers* of the New Testament (eg. love one another, forgive one another). In fact, when a person falls, for them it is an experience of loss and grieving. Isn't it our call to mourn with them? Rev. Jesse Jackson once said, "Never look down on anybody unless you are helping them up."[47]

Genuine empathy for the antagonists in our life is indeed a challenge, but it is doable with the Holy Spirit's help. You may be wondering; how do I personally meet this challenge? Well, I remind myself that...

- I must believe the best about people and their intentions.
- I am likely an antagonist in someone's eyes. How would I want them to treat me (Matthew 7:12)?
- Antagonists are loved by God and He watches over them just as he watches over me (Matthew 5:45). God would not be pleased with any mistreatment, nor with unkind thoughts.
- Very likely, my antagonists are engaged in a battle I know nothing about, but one that is negatively impacting their relationships and actions. Show grace.
- The Lord does not gloat when I fall. He seeks to redeem me and my situation. I should have the same desire for others (Ephesians 5:1).

My last word on how to treat the antagonists in our life who experience a fall is this: a healthy and growing disciple's response is always moving toward kindness (Galatians 5:22).

Be blessed, my friends.

Letter Twenty-Three

REFLECTIONS

Letters to my Friends

LETTER TWENTY-FOUR

#blessedtobeablessing

**OUR CALLING AS DISCIPLES IS TO
BE A BLESSING TO THE WORLD**

"The one who blesses others is abundantly blessed;
those who help others are helped."
Proverbs 11:25

"God does not need your good works, but your neighbour does."
Martin Luther

Hello Friends.

I have seen many *"#blessed"* social media references over the past year as people want to acknowledge the good in their life. As I have encountered them, few refer to being blessed by God and many are a form of self-glorification rather than glorifying God. What I have seen very little of are *"#blessedtobeablessing"* social media references. Perhaps this is the case because in our entitlement-oriented Canadian culture, this selfless, other-focused approach to life is not as appealing.

Being a blessing is living beyond ourselves in the service of others. A key mark of a spirit-filled disciple of Christ is the pouring out of one's life in sacrificial ways. Another perspective is that as followers of Jesus, the Holy Spirit has poured into us everything we need to be a blessing to others (Ephesians 1:13). Our gifts, divinely given, are to be shared. This is God's plan, and this is our responsibility in Christ Jesus.

To be a blessing is more than uttering a passing *"God bless you."* Rather, it is literally pouring ourselves into the well-being of another for the sake of Christ who emptied Himself for our salvation (Philippians 2:5).

Our motive for blessing others must be rooted in love – love for the Lord and love for others (Matthew 22:37-39). Reggie McNeal once said, "Every commonplace circumstance provides a heart-shaped opportunity."[48] So, by what tangible means can we be a blessing to others?

- WORDS – sharing the Gospel, giving praise, thanks, counsel and encouragement (Hebrews 3:13; 10:24).

- ✺ PRAYERS – asking the Father to give His favor, wisdom and help (James 5:16).
- ✺ PLANS – seeking another's best interests (Philippians 2:4).
- ✺ RESOURCES – giving material gifts (2 Corinthians 9:9ff; Matthew 25:35).
- ✺ ATTITUDE – displaying forbearance, patience, kindness (Galatians 5:22; Ephesians 4:32).
- ✺ THOUGHTS – thinking the best of another (Romans 12:10; 1 John 4:7).
- ✺ TIME – being present, lending a helping hand (Galatians 5:13; 1 Peter 4:10).

My final thought for now is this, hear in a fresh way the words of Jesus: "Let your light shine before men, that they may see your good works and give glory to your Father who is in heaven" (Matthew 5:16).

Be blessed, my friends.

Letters to my Friends

REFLECTIONS

LETTER TWENTY-FIVE

Ain't Jesus Somethin'

LESSONS FROM A SHOEHORN

"Serve wholeheartedly...."
Ephesians 6:7a

"True leadership must be for the benefit of the followers..."
John Maxwell

Hello Friends.

This week I was revisiting my journal, specifically the pages from the first days in my new ministry role. The journal entry from my first day on the job, so-to-speak, occurred during a pastor's retreat. Ron was the speaker. At the time he was serving in the national office with the Leaders to Leaders program. His counsel to us that day was practical and powerful.

Ron stated that when he travelled, he routinely took particular objects with him and pondered the life and faith lesson they could teach – this was the way of Jesus and so if it worked for the Lord, why not for him. He then pulled out a two-foot shoehorn and said it had something to teach us about ministry.

He began by having us wonder whether the disciples of Jesus didn't begin their ministry with the following attitude: *Ain't WE somethin'? We are the chosen few called to follow this cutting-edge rabbi! Look at us, folks!* However, over time, he surmised that their attitude was transformed to: *Ain't JESUS somethin! You are the Christ! Our Lord and our God!* The attitude of the disciples was transformed, in part, because of Jesus' example of servant leadership. He led out of love, seeking the wellbeing of others in all circumstances. The greatest is the servant of all. Ron suggested that our leadership must imitate that of Jesus and the shoehorn can help.

Ron said a shoehorn draws no attention to itself. In fact, it is often misplaced. A shoehorn exists to help others get into their shoes. A shoehorn helps the rich and poor, men and women, old and young, famous and infamous- it simply serves without question. A shoehorn has one simple (some would say, lowly) role, but it does it well. A shoehorn's identity is that of being a device to help people slip into their shoes. It was created for that task and lives it out day-after-day. It accomplishes its purpose, not on its own power, but through the strength of one greater than itself.

Ron was addressing Christian leaders in particular, but I believe his shoehorn lessons are applicable to all Christians. Like a shoehorn, a Christian needs to

- not draw attention to him/herself;
- delight in the need of another;
- seek out the least and serve them;
- look for, and do, lowly tasks; and
- serve from their identity in Christ.

I believe the following maxim captures the serving aspect of Ron's lesson well: *If serving is below you, leadership is beyond you.*

My friends, may Ron's shoehorn lesson bless your heart as it did mine.

PS. Ron, if you ever read this, I hope I accurately captured your message that day. I still have the shoehorn you gave me. Thank you for the wisdom. You not only shared it effectively, you modelled it too.

Be blessed, my friends.

REFLECTIONS

LETTER TWENTY-SIX

A Life Poured Out

LOVE IS NOT LOVE UNLESS YOU GIVE IT AWAY.

"...whoever loses his life for my sake will find it."
Matthew 10:39b

"If you want love and abundance in your life, give it away."
Mark Twain

Hello Friends.

Several years ago, I attended a city-wide prayer breakfast. The guest speaker was a godly educator named Gordon Elhard. Elhard had a passion for Jesus and a deep commitment to living and proclaiming the Gospel. What captivated my attention and heart were his closing words to the thousand-plus guests: "My mission is to give my life away." I immediately jotted down his words on a napkin, then in my personal journal. What brought his quote to mind recently was a Facebook post of a Sanskrit Proverb: "Rivers do not drink their own water; trees do not eat their own fruit; the sun does not shine on itself and flowers do not spread their fragrance for themselves. Living for others is a rule of nature. We are all born to help each other. No matter how difficult it is...Life is good when you are happy; but much better when others are happy because of you."

In my mind, both of these sentiments echo the words of the Apostle Paul to the church in Philippi, *"I am being poured out like a drink offering"* (Philippians 2:17). Here, I thought, is much to muse upon.

I have watched several episodes of the TV series called *Hoarders*. In full colour I see what happens to people when they set their lives upon themselves through the acquisition and hoarding of things. Without fail they experience relationship conflicts, become emotionally depleted, relationally dysfunctional and mentally distraught. The lesson I learned is that something breaks in us when we choose to invest our lives in ourselves rather than in others. I am not speaking of good healthy self-care, but the relentless pursuit of our own interests and happiness.

Letter Twenty-Six

The truth is we were created for a purpose beyond ourselves. The Westminster Catechism declares that the chief end of men and women is to "glorify God and to enjoy Him forever."[49] Jesus espoused that loving God and one's neighbour fulfills the law and prophets and by extension, our created purposes (Matthew 22:37-40). Our lives were made to be poured out for others and in so doing are blessed. This is a kingdom principle – a divine truth from our Creator supernaturally passed on to those made in His image. Blessed are they who live it out on their earthly pilgrimage.

As I grow older I become increasingly aware of the limited extent to which I have used my life to pour love and kindness into the lives of others. I have some deep regrets. I am also increasingly cognizant of the fact that, timewise, my proverbial cup has far less opportunity to be poured out. Our time is a non-renewable resource.

Jesus counselled us that in order to save our lives, we must give them up – pour them out for Him, the gospel and others (Mark 8:35). Dietrich Bonhoeffer maintained that, "When Christ calls a man, he bids him come and die."[50] Here is the ultimate call to sacrifice for another. Here is a discipleship metric.

As disciples we are recipients of a supernatural inner reservoir. Jesus refers to this fount as a "spring of water welling up to eternal life" and "streams of living water" (John 4:14; 7:38). This God-given 'water' is the Holy Spirit (John 7:39). The Spirit dwells in us. As a result, we have an unending divine fountain from which to pour out our lives for others.

Be blessed, my friends.

REFLECTIONS

LETTER TWENTY-SEVEN

Of Visions and Dreams

A SUPERNATURAL BLESSING

"In the last days, God says, I will pour out my Spirit on all people. Your sons and daughters will prophesy, your young men will see visions and your old men will dream dreams." Acts 2:17

"God visits us often, but most of the time we are not home."
French Proverb

Hello Friends.

I can still see it clearly in my mind, an old wooden watermill set deep in a grand forest close to a log cabin and powered by a bubbling brook. The sunshine is penetrating the tall majestic spruce, cedar and elm trees illuminating particular parts of the cabin, watermill and surrounding landscape. I seem to be able to smell the fragrance of the forest foliage and hear the babbling water as it runs along its course and moves the turbine paddles of the cedar mill. The singing of the birds is clear and melodic. I feel calm, at peace, in a space I'm supposed to be. And then, I awaken and it is gone. I journaled this revelation.

I don't experience many of these dreams, ones I can actually recount precisely a day later, I mean. There was something about this nocturnal reverie that spoke to my soul in a deeply profound way. I shared it with some close friends who have established history with dreams and visions. They listened closely and were kind in their commentary. They were helpful to point me in a direction, but wise enough to surrender the interpretation and application with me.

Six days later I found myself in northwest Saskatchewan preparing to meet with the members of a small-town church. They were celebrating the final Sunday with their pastor and entering into a time of transition. These were a handful of senior believers who would soon discuss their church's viability. Would they be able to call another pastor? Could they survive as a community of faith? I arrived at the church building, meeting the pastor and his wife. The plan was to gather the other members of the church at a home in the country a short distance away.

The log cabin where we were to fellowship was nestled in the forest. The sun was shining, illuminating the beauty of the setting. I exited my vehicle and the hosts immediately brought my attention to the forest fragrance, the sweet smell of country air and pristine foliage. I was given a tour of their cabin, filled with countless antiques and collectibles. And then, when I thought the experience could not get more idyllic, I saw through a window a large handmade wooden watermill. It was churning in the backyard beside a large babbling fountain which, if you closed your eyes, sounded exactly like a real cascading brook.

I shared some counsel with these believers from Psalm 139 about God having them close to His heart; that God would not abandon them during this time of loss and transition. I called them to be thankful in spite of their new realities and an uncertain future. I ended by sharing my watermill dream and pointed to the watermill not thirty feet away from where we were sitting. I intimated that my being there seemed divinely appointed. For several moments it was quiet, only the fountain and watermill could be heard. And then, the group, some with tears streaming down their faces, concluded – We think your presence and counsel at this exact time were meant to bring us peace, a sign that God is with us.

As I reflected upon this event, I was reminded of God's revelation to the prophet Isaiah: "For my thoughts are not your thoughts, neither are your ways my ways," declares the Lord. "As the heavens are higher than the earth, so are my ways higher than your ways and my thoughts than your thoughts" (Isaiah 55:8-9). God orchestrates his purposes in supernatural, and often mysterious, ways. Our response is to be one of faith and obedience.

May the Holy Spirit use your dreams and visions to bring shalom, hope, and joy into the spaces and times you find yourself.

Be blessed, my friends.

Letter Twenty-Seven

REFLECTIONS

Letters to my Friends

LETTER TWENTY-EIGHT

Sabbath

Letters to my Friends

Hello Friends.

Scripture repeatedly counsels followers of Jesus to wait upon the LORD. Too often we are in the rush of life, a place where no healthy spirituality can flourish. The psalmist writes, "Wait for the LORD; be still and take heart and wait for the LORD" (Psalm 27:14). *Faithful In The Wait* was inspired by Janine Renee and written May 12, 2015 at Evening Cove on Vancouver Island.

FAITHFUL IN THE WAIT

Be faithful in the wait my child,
Be strong, courageous, true.
Be still and let me chart the course,
For I'm preparing you.

It's in the wait the heart is shaped,
In quiet, vision fired.
It's in the still the soul is poised,
In quiet, hope inspired.

It's in the wait, cool waters soothe,
Fresh winds the spirit lifts.
It's in the still, passion burns,
The voice of doubt will drift.

Be faithful in the wait my child,
Where trust is tested pure.
Be still and know that I am God,
In me your joy is sure.

Letter Twenty-Eight

SABBATH PRAYER

Priest and theologian, Saint Ignatius of Loyola wrote, "Before all contemplations and meditations, there ought always to be made the preparatory prayer." During times of significant searching, wanting direction and discernment from God, I commit myself to times of listening – a most essential component of prayer. I adhere to the counsel of St. Loyola and carefully prepare my heart and soul. I need to center my whole being to one task, listening for the still small whisper of God. In some fashion, I employ *Waiting Prayer* for this task. This prayer was first put to paper on January 9, 2012, in Regina, Saskatchewan.

> "Do not be anxious about anything, but in everything
> by prayer and supplication with thanksgiving let
> your requests be made known to God."
> Philippians 4:6

> "Prayer should be the key of the day and the lock of the night."
> George Herbert

WAITING PRAYER

> Freely, in the stillness of this space, I open
>   my soul to you, O God.
> Holy Spirit, I welcome you, guide me in this
>   moment.
> Guard my heart and mind from the evil one.
> Demolish the inner walls I have constructed
>   against doing what pleases you.

Letter Twenty-Eight

Cast out any fear and all doubt that may
    impede the surrender of my heart.
Empower me to set aside my fleshly biases.
Prepare my spirit, O God, so that I might be
    fully present and available.
Help me release those temporary things that
    have consumed my thoughts.
Lord, grant me discernment to distill what
    I hear, wisdom to respond rightly.
Calm my soul, compose my mind, focus the
    eyes of my heart upon you.
Bless me with courage to forge my will into
    harmony with what you reveal.
O God, I am an untouched canvas awaiting
    your revelation, an empty scroll
    anticipating your words.
Amen.

REFLECTIONS

Letter Twenty-Eight

WEEK V

Letters to my Friends

LETTER TWENTY-NINE

Spiritual 'Mulligans'

THERE BUT FOR THE GRACE OF GOD, GO I.

"...one thing I do: Forgetting what is behind
and straining toward what is ahead, I press on...."
Paul, Philippians 3:13b-14a

"You can't go back and change the beginning,
but you can start where you are and change the ending."
C.S. Lewis

Hello Friends.

A "mulligan" is a golf term for a redemption stroke – a 'do-over.' It comes into play when your previous club stroke was embarrassingly terrible, in golf parlance, a "duff." I am an unashamed practitioner of the mulligan, with or without the knowledge or blessing of my golfing compadres. A mulligan allows me to shake off the fifty-yard 'worm-burner' and set my sights on a fresh attempt at reaching the green.

In his letter to the church in Philippi, the Apostle Paul recounts his religious pedigree and accomplishments and then sets them aside in favour of Christ and His salvific work. Paul's pre-Christ days were driven by a pharisaic works-for-salvation ethos. Now, however, he wants to forget this futile striving in favour of grace through faith in Christ – a religious do-over, a spiritual mulligan. Our own spiritual pilgrimage is likely far less dramatic than Paul's exploits from legalistic Pharisee to Spirit-filled ambassador for Christ. However, each of us have marched from some spiritual paradigm to life as a disciple of Jesus. By all accounts, an act of grace, right?

The longer I walk this discipleship course with Jesus, the greater an awareness of my need for spiritual 'mulligans.' Such do-overs are not as transforming as my life before and after Christ, but none-the-less, impactful. How many times have I landed in the 'rough' or in a proverbial sand trap as I plodded along the fairway of life God called me to play upon (1 John 2:6). At best, my walk with Jesus may be on par with his expectations, but my sense is that I serve with a 'handicap', sometimes driving myself into a triple 'bogey.' In this regard, I derive hope from Scripture's counsel: "If we confess our sins, he is faithful and just and will forgive us our sins and purify us from all unrighteousness" (1 John 1:9). In addition, a slice of the gospel narrative that I find genuinely inspiring is the story of Peter's betrayal of Jesus, and his subsequent redemption (John 18 & 21). If Jesus offered Peter a spiritual 'mulligan' for betrayal, will He not freely extend one to us when we make discipleship 'duffs'? The answer, in my case, is an overwhelming "yes." Amazing grace.

A fascinating story is told about the origins of the phrase, *"There but for the grace of God, go I."* According to phrases.org this adage was "first spoken by the English evangelical preacher and martyr, John Bradford (circa 1510–1555). He is said to have uttered the variant of the expression - "There but for the grace of God, goes John Bradford," when seeing criminals being led to the scaffold." Bradford's insight points me to God's grace in my own life. The 'spiritual mulligans' I have been blessed with were amazing and have redeemed my relationship with Jesus and kept me from trudging into genuinely harmful destructive moral and spiritual predicaments.

Peter's redemption and Bradford's quote are perhaps weighty illustrations to make my simple proposition that spiritual 'mulligans' are an indispensable part of one's walk with Jesus. Discipleship is not a game or a science, or even an art; it is a relational venture where one can supernaturally grow into Christlikeness. It is seasoned with a multitude of blessings, but also peppered with 'hazards.' Thanks be to God for his grace should we reap the first and avoid the second. Thanks be to God for his grace – for spiritual 'mulligans' – when a discipleship 'duff' occurs.

    Postscriptum (PS): To any serious golfer reading this piece, I am aware that a professional golf game does not allow for mulligans. Too bad, as I believe there are a few golf pros who could remember a time when they would have welcomed one.

Be blessed, my friends.

Letter Twenty-Nine

REFLECTIONS

Letters to my Friends

LETTER THIRTY

"$3 Worth Of God" People

CHRIST'S CROSS DEMANDS GREAT SACRIFICE

"And he died for all, that those who live should no longer
live for themselves but for him who died for them and
was raised again."
2 Corinthians 5:15

"When Christ calls a man, he bids him come and die."
Dietrich Bonhoeffer

Hello Friends.

Wilbur E. Rees was an American pastor who wrote a devotional titled *$3 Worth Of God* published in 1971. I tried to get a copy of his work and discovered it was a Christian literary collectible. In his book he shares a sentiment used in countless sermons; a reflection pertaining to the depth of some believer's engagement with God.

> "I would like to buy $3 worth of God please, not enough to explode my soul or disturb my sleep, but just enough to equal a cup of warm milk or a snooze in the sunshine. I don't want enough of him to make me love a black man or pick beets with a migrant. I want ecstasy, not transformation; I want the warmth of the womb, not a new birth. I want a pound of the eternal in a paper sack. I would like to buy $3 dollars worth of God please."[51]

Jesus' call upon a disciple's life is in stark contrast to pursuing just $3 worth of God:

> "If you love your father or mother more than you love me, you are not worthy of being mine; or if you love your son or daughter more than me, you are not worthy of being mine. If you refuse to take up your cross and follow me, you are not worthy of being mine" (Matthew 10:37-38 NLT).

> *"Then Jesus said to his disciples, "If any of you wants to be my follower, you must give up your own way, take up your cross, and follow me"* (Matthew 16:24 NLT).

> "...any of you who does not give up everything he has cannot be my disciple" (Luke 14:33).

The cost of being a disciple is high and Jesus counseled those considering such a path to count the sacrifice (Luke 14:28-32).

In his classic work, , German pastor and theologian Dietrich Bonhoeffer wrote:

> "Costly grace is the gospel which must be sought again and again, the gift which must be asked for, the door at which a man must knock. Such grace is costly because it calls us to follow, and it is grace because it calls us to follow Jesus Christ. It is costly because it costs a man his life, and it is grace because it gives a man the only true life. It is costly because it condemns sin, and grace because it justifies the sinner. Above all, it is costly because it cost God the life of his Son: "ye were bought at a price," and what has cost God much cannot be cheap for us. Above all, it is grace because God did not reckon his Son too dear a price to pay for our life, but delivered him up for us. Costly grace is the Incarnation of God."[52]

Do we as followers of Jesus genuinely know much about the actual cost of discipleship? Do we fathom the costly grace that Bonhoeffer speaks of? Do you sense that believers are pursuing self-indulgence more than the cross of Christ? Have we allowed the god of hedonism to usurp Christ's rightful place in our hearts? Are we *$3 worth of God* people?

When I survey the wondrous cross
On which the Prince of glory died,
My richest gain I count but loss,
And pour contempt on all my pride.

Forbid it, Lord, that I should boast,
Save in the death of Christ my God!
All the vain things that charm me most,
I sacrifice them to His blood.

See from His head, His hands, His feet,
Sorrow and love flow mingled down!
Did e'er such love and sorrow meet,
Or thorns compose so rich a crown?

Were the whole realm of nature mine,
That were a present far too small;
Love so amazing, so divine,
Demands my soul, my life, my all.[53]

Isaac Watts, 1707

Be blessed, my friends.

Letter Thirty

REFLECTIONS

Letters to my Friends

LETTER THIRTY-ONE

Uncommon Moments

THINGS CHANGE WHEN GOD BREAKS INTO OUR SPACE

"As thou knowest not what is the way of the spirit,
nor how the bones do grow in the womb of her that is with child:
even so thou knowest not the works of God who maketh all."
Ecclesiastes 11:5 KJV

"Be ready for the Lord's surprise visits."
Oswald Chambers

Hello Friends.

The life of a disciple is filled with common moments, everyday spaces where the ordinary and routine abide. This is a gift of God. Here disciples must be disciplined, resilient and faithful to the person and mission of Jesus. Here is where an enhanced dedication to godliness and holiness must prevail. In the common moment is where the primary work of discipleship is done. Every disciple will reside, so-to-speak, in this common plain of life, occasionally taking hikes to the proverbial spiritual mountain tops or tumbling down into the spiritual valleys. These sojourns too, are gifts of God.

Breaking into the common moments are divine encounters. Sooner or later all disciples experience these supernatural interventions. Uncommon moments serve specific purposes in shaping the disciple. Often they are, at least initially, mysterious and unexplainable, but with time, and after seeking revelation from God, their purpose becomes known. The following are two of my uncommon moments:

> Three friends and I were barreling down a hill in Abbotsford in 1980 with a sharp right hand turn less than fifty feet away. I had accelerated my car past 100 kilometers per hour. I was already visualizing brakes squealing, the car crossing the median and careening into a concrete barrier on the opposite side of the street. Unlike previous accidents I had racked up, this one would involve friends and result in serious damage. I braced myself for the impact. Moments later, with the engine running and all of us in the car dead quiet, none of us knew what happened or how it

happened. We were on the other side of the concrete barrier, idling in a vacant parking lot. No one spoke of the event and I'm not sure why. Looking back I believe we all knew that a divine intervention had happened and speaking of it somehow seemed to violate something sacred.

This particular uncommon moment forged a deep impression upon my life. Specifically, I felt like Jeremiah, that I was being set apart for a kingdom purpose. God formed me, knew me, and was protecting me from harm in order for his appointed purpose to be fulfilled in my life. This was not about me, but about God's purposes, of which I played a part. This uncommon moment was the catalyst for a five year quest of discerning how God's blueprint included me. Thirty-eight years later a second uncommon moment.

> It was 2018 and early on a frigid and dark winter morning as I traveled alone to Saskatoon. I was just about ten kilometres south of a village called Chamberlain, forty-five minutes north of Regina. Heart-stopping. That was what it felt like. Directly in front of my speeding rental car, standing across the entire roadway, a herd of white-tailed deer! I was too close to jam on the brakes knowing that doing so would lower the nose of the vehicle and lift a deer through the windshield. Closing my eyes I prepared for the awful impact. Seconds passed. Nothing but quiet. Several more seconds passed. I looked up into the rear-view mirror. All I could see, beside the passing roadway, was deer continuing to cross. I could not explain how my vehicle passed through a herd of deer unscathed.

This uncommon moment also left a remarkable imprint upon me. I was now in my twenty-seventh year of vocational ministry. This God moment reminded me of his presence and protection, and that there continued to be a kingdom purpose for my life. This uncommon moment granted me greater confidence of God's blessing upon the ministry I was engaged in and his protection for carrying it out. This experience also served as a significant encouragement to those with whom I shared it.

Pastor and author Henry Blackaby claimed that God's people live by divine revelation. Supernatural encounters, like the uncommon moments I've described should move disciples to seek the purpose of God in the present moment.[54] When they do so, their lives are never the same again. For example, when the Lord interrupted Saul's common moments it led to the pharisee's transformed life (Acts 9). Following his conversion the Christian community exploded in growth and impact. Saul the church persecutor became Paul the Jesus proclaimer. The world would never be the same again.

God is in the business of breaking into the everyday routines of a disciple's life to reveal, confront, encourage or call. Wise is one who responds to these uncommon moments with simple faith, submission and obedience. I resonate deeply with young Samuel's response to his own experience of God breaking into his life, "Speak [Lord], for your servant is listening" (1 Samuel 3:10b). Here is a heart that God can transform. Such a transformed heart impacts community. Samuel grew to be a powerful prophet, a man of God who anointed King David. And, this royal forever changed the culture and spirituality of Israel.

In his classic work, *My Utmost For His Highest*, Oswald Chambers writes, "Jesus rarely comes where we expect Him; He appears where we least expect Him, and always in the most illogical connections. The only way a worker can keep true to God is by being ready for the Lord's surprise visits."[55] What does being ready for God's surprise visits entail? Chambers maintains it is by being "spiritually real." My sense is that being spiritually real means living day-to-day expecting the Lord to speak and act in the common moments of my life. And, when he does, responding in faith with submission and obedience. If we live with the expectation that God is speaking into our lives, we will no doubt find that God literally 'appears' – in both common and uncommon moments. It is my responsibility and my joy to allow those moments to transform me and my world.

Be blessed, my friends.

Letters to my Friends

REFLECTIONS

LETTER THIRTY-TWO

Safety Labels, Indiana Jones and Wisdom

INSIGHT FOR ENGAGING A BROKEN NEW WORLD

"The fear of the Lord is the foundation of wisdom."
Psalm 111:10a (NLT)

"Two things are infinite. The universe and human stupidity.
And I'm not so sure about the universe."
Attributed to Albert Einstein

"Choose wisely."
Holy Grail Knight's advice to Indiana Jones
Indiana Jones and the Last Crusade

Hello Friends.

Some time ago I read an article where the author was sharing his findings after studying safety labels on merchandise. He described this venture as being quite humourous. Some of the examples he used to make his point included:

- On a hair dryer: Do not use while sleeping.
- On a bar of soap: Use like regular soap.
- On a sleeping aid: Warning: May cause drowsiness.
- On a chain saw: Do not attempt to stop chain with your hands.
- On a child's superhero costume: Wearing of this garment does not enable you to fly.

I must admit, I chuckled. If safety labels like these are required, I wonder how long the human race can survive. There seems to be a definite dearth of common sense among homo sapiens. Humour aside, we face a very serious and expanding problem among us: a lack of wisdom. My seminary professor Tremper Longman III said that wisdom is a knowing how – that is, knowing how to navigate life. According to Longman, wisdom (hokma in Hebrew) is "...the skill of living. It is practical knowledge that helps one know how to act and how to speak in different situations. Wisdom entails the ability to avoid problems, and the skill to handle them when they present themselves."[56] Wisdom is the ability to avoid life's pitfalls and reap life's blessings. Wisdom is not intelligence, per say, but includes it. Theologically,

Letter Thirty-Two

Anglican Priest Tripp Prince claims that "Wisdom is the knowledge of God and a life lived for God."[57]

More and more I see a lack of *knowing how* in the church. Although wisdom is often preached about and prayed for, I'm not sure the church is doing what is necessary to possess *hokma*.

Why is this pertinent for the church? Today the church is in a situation of unique realities:

- The pandemic caused churches to evolve quickly to find creative and engaging ways to worship corporately outside of an in-person format. What is the best long-term solution for meeting the pastoral needs of all church attendees?
- The discovery of unmarked graves on former residential school sites fueled anti-church sentiments toward Catholic and Protestant faith communities. What is our role in reconciliation?
- A growing number of research studies report a significant loss of trust in pastors, priests and churchgoers among the unchurched. How do we restore this lost faith?
- There is an emergence of hyper-individualism, racial conflict, religious intolerance, and gender identity confusion. How do we speak into these issues?
- The phenomenal rise in burnout, PTSD and depression among disciples of Jesus is concerning. How can we help the affected heal?

My point is that the church will need much wisdom to navigate these and other profound challenges. The good news is that unlimited wisdom is available to disciples (and by extension the Church) who are serious about obtaining it.

It has been forty years since the first Indiana Jones movie came out. Who didn't want to be like Indiana Jones – handsome, intelligent, and courageous? And, talk about adventure in foreign lands with awesome jungles, caves, snakes and people. Makes me want to watch it again! For me, the most memorable thing about the movie was Indiana's passion and drive. Nothing would keep him from finding the Ark of the Covenant because he understood its precious and powerful nature. I believe I need to pursue wisdom like Indiana pursued this ancient artifact. Consider the Bible's counsel: "Wisdom is supreme; therefore, get wisdom. Though it cost all you have, get understanding" (Proverbs 4:7). "Wisdom is more precious than rubies, and nothing you desire can compare with her" (Proverbs 8:11).

In his search for the historic ark, Indiana Jones followed a series of clues which he had recorded in his personal leather-bound journal. Similarly, the Bible gives us clues. As followers of Christ, a primary source in our search for wisdom is his written word: "All Scripture is inspired by God and is useful to teach us what is true and to make us realize what is wrong in our lives. It corrects us when we are wrong and teaches us to do what is right. God uses it to prepare and equip his people to do very good work" (2 Timothy 3:16-17 NLT). It also serves to anchor us in an unchanging hope and joy. Charles Spurgeon once said, "A Bible that's falling apart usually belongs to someone who isn't."

So, what clues does Scripture offer concerning the obtaining of wisdom?

- Honour God and obey His commands – "The fear of the Lord is the foundation of true wisdom. All who obey [God's] commandments will grow in wisdom" (Psalm 111:10 NLT).
- Allow God to help you know yourself (Psalm 139:23-24; Lamentations 3:40; 2 Corinthians 13:5).
- Learn from life experiences, especially mistakes (Psalm 90:12; Proverbs 24:30-34).
- Acquire insight from godly wise people – "Walk with the wise and become wise" (Proverbs 13:20).
- Ask God for it – "If you need wisdom, ask our generous God, and he will give it to you" (James 1:5 NLT, Proverbs 2:6).

If we stopped here, the Preacher (usually identified as King Solomon) in the Old Testament book of Ecclesiastes would caution us about pursuing wisdom simply to gain wisdom. He is right; pursuing wisdom for itself is vanity. There must be a greater good one is seeking – a higher value, a purpose beyond ourselves. God is that greater good and we pursue wisdom to please him and align ourselves with his will. Furthermore, the Preacher did not know of Jesus. If he had known Jesus, I am convinced he would declare that all the treasures of knowledge and wisdom are found in Jesus. Such a claim would be in harmony with the Apostle Paul's assertion that Jesus is the *"wisdom of God"* (1 Corinthians 1:24,30; Colossians 2:3). Christ Jesus is the higher and greater 'good' we seek in our pursuit of wisdom. As disciples, ultimately our quest for wisdom will lead us back to Jesus; he is the fullest revelation of God's wisdom.

I have much hope that individual disciples and the

collective Body of Christ will recommit themselves to a pursuit of biblical and godly wisdom. Furthermore, I continue to be convinced that disciples need to pursue wisdom like Indiana Jones pursued the biblical Ark. Such a quest will likewise be filled with adventures.

Whatever our life circumstance, if we want to avoid life's pitfalls and reap life's blessings, my initial counsel is to love God with all our heart, soul and mind and follow the instruction he provides in His Word. As the Preacher surveyed his life he declared "Here now is my final conclusion: Fear God and obey his commands, for this is everyone's duty" (Ecclesiastes 12:13b NLT). On this side of the cross, my counsel is to look to Jesus, the wisdom of God incarnate. Jesus not only helps us navigate life's pitfalls, but he is also the One who gives us right standing with God when we stumble into one of those pitfalls (1 Corinthians 1:30). Jesus helps us reap life's blessings, but even more than that, he is the source of them (Philippians 4:19).

Be blessed, my friends.

Letter Thirty-Two

REFLECTIONS

Letters to my Friends

LETTER THIRTY-THREE

The Making of a Good Day

THANKS-LIVING: THE DISCIPLE'S POSTURE

"Give thanks in all circumstances,
for this is God's will for you in Christ Jesus."
1 Thessalonians 5:18

"Each day is God's gift to you.
What you do with it is your gift to Him."
T.D. Jakes

Hello Friends.

I know that this dates me somewhat, but I grew up (and loved) singing the old classic chorus *This Is The Day*. Here are some of the lyrics:

> This is the day, this is the day.
> That the Lord has made, that the Lord has made.
> We will rejoice, we will rejoice,
> And be glad in it, and be glad in it.
> This is the day that the Lord has made.
> We will rejoice and be glad in it.
> This is the day, this is the day
> That the Lord has made.

The conviction I am to impress upon my heart from this song is a simple one – because the Lord made this day (every day), I am to rejoice and be glad. If I am truthful, I struggle at times with that conviction. Sometimes my day is a royal pain from beginning to end! Some days I feel more like ranting than rejoicing; more like grumbling than being glad. For me, not every day feels like a good day, even though God, whom I love deeply, has made it and is allowing me to experience it (Psalm 139:16). Still, at the end of a day I identify more with Shakespeare's character Macbeth: "Tomorrow, and tomorrow, and tomorrow, Creeps on this petty pace from day to day...."[58] Ever feel like that?

A man attending a very popular motivational seminar was asked by its world-renowned speaker whether or not he was successful. "Absolutely!" the man responded with a huge grin. "Why is that?" the speaker asked him."

"It's so easy. All I have to do is get up, look down, and see that I am above ground! Every day above ground is a great day!"[59]

How do you feel about that? Is everyday above ground a great day? I once prayed faithfully for a grade eleven student who broke his back in a motorcycle accident. He spent months in hospital and rehab. Today he is in a wheelchair. Do you think the day of his accident was for him a great day simply because he was above ground? Perhaps. Is today a good day for him simply because he is above ground? Perhaps. Does simply being alive make for a good day? If not, what is it that makes a good day good; a day for which we can be thankful regardless of the experiences of it?

One personal reflection about what makes a good day good involves the opportunity to chase my dreams. Martin Luther King Jr. famously proclaimed, "I have a dream."[60] George Bernard Shaw said, "Some men see things as they are and say "Why?" I dream things that never were and say "Why not?"[61] We all have dreams, something we want to accomplish or experience that will make us say, "I did it...I really did it!" The truth is that until your heart actually stops beating your dreams are waiting to be fulfilled. But here's the thing, we need time to do them and occasion to reach that dream. And so, my thought is that I can be thankful and rejoice when I wake up to a new day because it provides me a chance to pursue my life goals. That's a good day.

Opportunity is not just about dreams; it is also about the chance to make things right. Some time ago, I came across *If Tomorrow Never Comes* and it really struck a chord with me. This poem points me to another reason I should consider rejoicing over each day:

IF TOMORROW NEVER COMES

If I knew it would be the last time that I'd see you fall
asleep, I would tuck you in more tightly and pray the Lord, your
soul to keep. If I knew it would be the last time that I see you
walk out the door, I would give you a hug and kiss and call you
back for one more....

For surely there's always tomorrow to make up for an oversight,
and we always get a second chance to make everything right.
There will always be another day to say our "I love you's." And
certainly there's another chance to say our "Anything I can do's?"

But just in case I might be wrong, and today is all I get, I'd like to
say how much I love you and I hope we never forget, Tomorrow
is not promised to anyone, young or old alike, And today may be
the last chance you get to hold your loved one tight."
(Author Unknown)

My younger brother Edward died of cancer. It was a horrible, painful, soul-crushing death as the cancerous tumors literally broke his bones and disfigured his body. Before he was admitted to hospital I traveled to B.C. to visit him at his home. Our relationship before this visit was not meaningful; cordial at best. Somehow the visit devolved and he became incensed about our conversation. He demanded that I leave. I flew home sick about how the visit ended. He would not take my follow-up calls. After he was admitted to the hospital and I was informed that his death was approaching, through another family member I asked for permission to visit him. He agreed. My heart sank when I saw his now crumpled body connected to multiple tubes. That day, I asked him to forgive me for anything I said or did that caused him offense and hurt. He forgave me. I told him that I loved him.

That day at the hospital was a good day. Although my brother was suffering and on his deathbed, although his family was devastated, although my own heart was broken and grieving over all the guilt of lost years of relationship, I could be thankful and rejoice because God gave me an opportunity to reconcile. We started a new relationship that day, albeit only days in length. The epilogue to this story is that Ed's family asked me to officiate his funeral. I felt honoured.

The Bible counsels: *"As we have opportunity, let us do good to all people, especially to those who belong to the family of believers"* (Galatians 6:9-10). Every day that God gifts to us provides an opportunity for us be difference-makers for joy in someone's day. To me, such an opportunity makes for a good day, one for which I can be thankful and glad about.

Is there someone you can think of who could use a hug from you? Is there someone you can think of right now who would love you to take them out for a coffee and just talk to them? Is there someone that comes to your mind who would smile from ear to ear should you come by and say, *"I can help you with that. Let me do that for you."* Consider the following sentiment I discovered:

This is the beginning of a new day.
You have been given this day
to use as you will...
You can waste it or use it for good.
What you do today is important because
you are exchanging a day of your life for it.
When tomorrow comes, this day will be gone forever.
In its place is something you have left behind...
Let it be something good.
—*Unknown*

What makes a good day good is that it comes from a good God and is imbued with opportunity for good. For that I am thankful. This is to be the posture of a disciple, a posture of thanks-living. This is the day that the Lord has made, and I will be glad and rejoice in it.

Be blessed, my friends.

Letter Thirty-Three

REFLECTIONS

Letters to my Friends

LETTER THIRTY-FOUR

God's 'Enoughness'

WHEN ALL YOU CAN DO IS LOOK UP

"The Lord is my Shepherd, I lack nothing."
Psalm 23:1a NET

"He who has God and everything else,
Has no more than he who has only God."
C.S. Lewis

Letters to my Friends

Hello Friends.

I first heard the expression *God's 'enoughness'* during a Zoom webinar focused on helping church leaders cope with the challenges of leadership during the COVID pandemic. It stuck with me ever since. I jotted down this expression in my journal that day and added notes about it in the weeks that followed. For example, in my study of Genesis seventeen, I came across some reflections from Dr. John MacArthur in his book *Our Sufficiency In Christ*:

> "One of the Old Testament names of God is El Shaddai, meaning "the All-Sufficient One." It is a name rich with meaning. Those who worship Him in Spirit and in truth find Him adequate for every necessity of life. They do not need any supplementary experience, a stronger dose of His redemption, or any other spiritual or emotional accoutrements. God has given to every believer abundant grace that is utterly sufficient to fulfill our deepest longings, our most intense cravings, our most profound needs – every human requirement."[62]

In subsequent devotional times, I read the following counsel from Scripture:

"...my God will meet all your needs according to the riches of his glory in Christ Jesus" (Philippians 4:19).

"My grace is sufficient for you" (2 Corinthians 12:9) or as another Bible version reads: "My grace is enough; it's all you need" (MSG.).

"His divine power has given us everything we need for

a godly life through our knowledge of him who called us by his own glory and goodness" (2 Peter 1:3).

It wasn't long before I came across a poem by the Catholic mystic St. Teresa Avila:

GOD ALONE IS ENOUGH

> Let nothing upset you,
> let nothing startle you.
> All things pass;
> God does not change.
> Patience wins
> all it seeks.
> Whoever has God
> lacks nothing:
> God alone is enough."[63]

And then, as I was reciting Psalm 23 as part of my prayer time, I was halted when I said aloud the words *"The Lord is my Shepherd, I shall not want (KJV)."* I had recited this line thousands of times but on that day these words struck a new chord in my spirit, *I shall not want.* Another Bible version reads *I lack nothing.*

At first glance this seems simplistic given all the realities of life and human nature. But then faith is intended to be simple in the midst of all the complexities of walking through time and space on this earth. David's sentiments in Psalm 23 moved me to revisit God's 'enoughness.'

I am unwavering in my confession that God is sovereign, that he knows me and my needs, and that he treats me as his beloved. Similarly, I am anchored to Jesus' counsel that the Heavenly Father will take care of me and my needs if I seek first the Kingdom of God (Matthew 6). All this being said, do I genuinely believe that I lack nothing, that God is enough for all my life, all of my needs, all of my hopes and dreams?

If I reflect upon my life of fifty some years, I would conclude that God has indeed met my needs; his grace has been sufficient. My expectations may not have been met but I am actually thankful they weren't because most were selfish and ill-considered. My hopes were sometimes dashed but again, if they had been fulfilled, I very likely would have found myself outside of God's best for me. I constantly find it amazing how my life's most difficult experiences have been ones in which I was reminded of, and experienced, God's 'enoughness.'

I am not a deep thinker, great theologian or capable philosopher, however, I know in my bones that in all of my travels and travails, God has been sufficient. With my Shepherd, I lack nothing.

Be blessed, my friends.

Letter Thirty-Four

REFLECTIONS

Letters to my Friends

LETTER THIRTY-FIVE

Sabbath

Hello Friends.

"My times are in your hands," (Psalm 31:15a) wrote the ancient psalmist as he proclaimed his trust in the Lord. His hope and refuge was in His sovereign God. *My Times* was written on June 29, 2015 in Regina, Saskatchewan after a time of reflection and meditation of Psalm 31. It was revised in 2021.

MY TIMES

> My times are in your hands Lord,
> Their ways an open scroll.
> All things I plan and purpose,
> Are scripted in your roll.
>
> No days of mine are hidden,
> No hour out of sight.
> Each movement of my spirit,
> Is brought into your light.

Letter Thirty-Five

My pilgrimage is shadowed,
Each step a guarded plot.
A sojourn not forsaken,
A path divinely wrought.

My times are in your hands Lord,
I cast out doubt and fear.
I march ahead undaunted,
Your presence always near.

Letters to my Friends

SABBATH PRAYER

While in Ladysmith, British Columbia, I wrote *Be My Divine Compass, A Prayer* as a way of tangibly acknowledging my need for a divine direction-giver in my life. This divine compass is the Holy Spirit of God. He is not only the one who helps me to travel well in this life, he also empowers me to live a life pleasing to him. As a follower of Christ I am mindful of the Lord's words to his disciples, "…when he, the Holy Spirit comes, he will guide you into all truth" (John 16:13).

> "In your unfailing love you will lead the people
> you have redeemed. In your strength you
> will guide them to your holy dwelling."
> Exodus 15:13

> "Guidance, like all God's acts of blessing under
> the covenant of grace, is a sovereign act."
> J.I. Packer

BE MY DIVINE COMPASS, A PRAYER

Holy Spirit, be my divine compass,
    my direction-giver.
Point me aright on this path of pilgrimage,
    this road of sacred devotion.
Direct my way on this earthly plain,
    set my feet true.
Guide me onto paths of love, truth and grace,
    reset my course should I wander.

Letter Thirty-Five

Keep me from destructive trails,
> navigate me away from selfish pursuits.

Whether east, west, north or south,
> lead me to what you have purposed.

Amen.

REFLECTIONS

Letter Thirty-Five

WEEK VI

Letters to my Friends

LETTER THIRTY-SIX

Crooked Thinking

**AVOIDING TWISTED DISCERNMENT
IN A WARPED CULTURE**

"One cannot think crooked and walk straight."
Unknown

"Trust in the Lord with all your heart
and lean not on your own understanding;
in all your ways acknowledge him,
and he will make your paths straight."
Proverbs 3:5-6

Hello Friends.

Saskatchewan is home to a botanical mystery – the Crooked Trees. Also called the Crooked Bush, this three-acre grove of kinked Aspen trees is located an hour west of Saskatoon, near the village of Hafford. The trees are said to have developed a genetic mutation that makes their growth a twisted aberration. This unique tourist attraction nestled in rural Saskatchewan reminds me of a Dr. Suess story setting. It also brings to my mind a claim by Dallas Willard in his book *Renovation of the Heart: Putting on the Character of Christ*:

> "The prospering of God's cause on earth depends upon his people thinking well...Bluntly, to serve God well we must think straight; and crooked thinking, unintentional or not, always favors evil. And when crooked thinking gets elevated into group orthodoxy, whether religious or secular; there is, quite literally, 'hell to pay.'"[64]

As disciples of Jesus, we want to be a people who think straight in a crooked culture, we want to be biblically anchored thinkers. Our theological heritage as Mennonite Brethren, as evangelical Anabaptists, is one that gives witness to such conviction. Consider, for example, the words of Menno Simons in 1539: "We certainly hope no one of rational mind will be so foolish a man as to deny that the whole Scriptures both Old and New Testament, were written for our instruction, admonition, and correction, and that they are the true scepter and rule by which the Lord's kingdom, house, church, and congregation must be ruled and governed."[65] Through the centuries, the descendants of Anabaptists, including Mennonite Brethren, have held to a bibliocentric faith. Scripture governed all aspects of both faith and life. They would assert that straight (godly) thinking was always connected to biblical thinking and departure from the same would lead one to crooked thinking.

Why am I writing about crooked and straight (biblical) thinking? I am penning my thoughts here because as disciples we are constantly being tempted to primarily 'weigh' what our culture promotes outside of biblical thinking. Our culture tends to champion a worldview that is has no space for the God of Scripture, epitomizes self-worship, and denounces any claim to absolute truth. Ours is a culture that sees the Bible as an impediment to self-love, which in reality is code for hedonism. Social media mantras like "Your truth above all truth," "Be the perfect you," "You can do anything," "Just do it," and "One love" are just a sampling of this reality. In our times, disciples need to return to biblical thinking to avoid crooked thinking.

In this 21st century, what I discovered helpful as a disciple of Jesus is Scripture's counsel for me to:

SEEK the help of the Holy Spirit
"Search me, O God, and know my heart; test me and know my thoughts. See if there is any wicked way in me, and lead me in the way everlasting"
(Psalm 139:23-24 NRSV).

SURRENDER crooked thinking
"Don't copy the behavior and customs of this world, but let God transform you into a new person by changing the way you think. Then you will learn to know God's will for you, which is good and pleasing and perfect"
(Romans 12:2 NLT).

"We demolish arguments and every pretension that sets itself up against the knowledge of God, and we take captive every thought to make it obedient to Christ" (2 Corinthians 10:5).

SET your thinking on Christ
"Because [Jesus] himself suffered when he was tempted, he is able to help those who are being tempted. Therefore, holy brothers [and sisters], who share in the heavenly calling, fix your thoughts on Jesus, whom we acknowledge as our apostle and high priest"
(Hebrews 2:18-3:1).

SUBSTITUTE crooked thinking with straight (godly) thinking.
"Finally, brothers [and sisters], whatever is true, whatever is noble, whatever is right, whatever is pure, whatever is lovely, whatever is admirable—if anything is excellent or praiseworthy—think about such things"
(Philippians 4:8).

"Think about the things of heaven, not the things of earth" (Colossians 3:2 NLT).

Letter Thirty-Six

The Apostle Paul, writing to the church in Philippi taught them to live like Christ "in a warped and crooked generation" (Philippians 1:21; 2:15). We are to do the same. The crooked generation of Paul's time is well and alive today. The Scriptures serve as a fundamental catalyst for the disciple of Christ to be his life-transforming presence in the world: "All Scripture is God-breathed and is useful for teaching, rebuking, correcting and training in righteousness, so that the servant of God may be thoroughly equipped for every good work (2 Timothy 3:16-17 NIV). Disciples are to think biblically as we encounter the messaging of our culture and not adopt the self-absorbed humanistic philosophies of our generation. Scripture is to be our inspired rubric so-to-speak; our supernatural counselor: "For the word of God is alive and active. Sharper than any double-edged sword, it penetrates even to dividing soul and spirit, joints and marrow; it judges the thoughts and attitudes of the heart" (Hebrews 4:12 NIV).

Crooked thinking is not to find a home in the life of a disciple of Jesus. We are to avoid twisted discernment in a warped culture. In contrast, we are to possess the mind of Christ (1 Corinthians 2:16). "Those are Christians who are minded as Christ was," wrote Hans Schaffer in 1527[66] In 1537 Simons echoed this sentiment when he penned that we are to be "of the same mind as Christ, walk as he did."[67] Jesus' thinking was in tune with the Holy Spirit, obedient to the Father and anchored to the Scripture (biblical thinking). May the Lord give us all wisdom in these matters.

Be blessed, my friends.

Letters to my Friends

REFLECTIONS

LETTER THIRTY-SEVEN

Dear Discouraged

THE ROLE OF LIST-MAKING IN DISPELLING DISCOURAGEMENT

"Nobody is okay all the time."
Star Trek: Discovery

"But now trouble comes to you,
and you are discouraged;
it strikes you, and you are dismayed."
Job 4:5

Hello Friends.

I journal. One of my writing practices is to create lists in my journal. For example, I routinely pen lists about my blessings or concerning people and things I want to pray for or things I want to stop or start. Frankly, I have a boat load of lists. Apparently, the unflattering technical terms associated with compulsive list-making are *listophile, listomaniac* and *listoholic*. Before you pigeonhole me as an overly zealous *listographer*, I've done the online assessments regarding those who are somewhat regimented about list-making and I'm in the healthy 'normal' category. I'm being tongue in cheek.

Seriously, I have discovered that creating lists is cathartic, grounding, inspiring and therapeutic. For example, and to the point of this writing, when I feel discouraged, the following lists (which are still expanding) help me gain perspective on my troubles and routinely serve to be uplifting.

SCRIPTURAL INSPIRATION FOR TIMES OF DISCOURAGEMENT:

OLD TESTAMENT	NEW TESTAMENT	JESUS
Deuteronomy 31:8	Romans 8:31-39	Matthew 6:25ff
Joshua 1:6-9	1 Corinthians 15:58	Matthew 6:34
Psalm 23	2 Corinthians 4:16-18	Matthew 7:7-8
Psalm 121	Ephesians 6:10	Matthew 7:24-25

Letter Thirty-Seven

Isaiah 41:10	Philippians 1:6	Matthew 11:28
Jeremiah 29:11	Philippians 4:6-13	Matthew 14:27
Zephaniah 3:17	1 Peter 5:7	Matthew 28:2

REALIZATION ABOUT BIBLICAL CHARACTERS WHOSE TROUBLES WERE WORSE THAN MINE:

- ADAM & EVE – thrown out of paradise
- JOB – lost farm, finances, family and health
- JONAH – swallowed by a whale
- SAMSON – had his eyes gouged out
- DANIEL – thrown into a den of lions
- RUTH – husband died
- JOHN – exiled to an island

AWARENESS ABOUT BIBLICAL CHARACTERS WHOSE CHALLENGES WERE GREATER THAN MINE:

- NOAH – building a mammoth ark
- JOSHUA – filling the shoes of Moses
- DAVID – rebuilding his reputation after committing adultery and murder
- NEHEMIAH – orchestrating the building of Jerusalem's walls
- ESTHER – finding a way to save the Jews from Haman's evil plot
- PETER – dealing with his betrayal of Jesus
- PAUL – living with the fact that he persecuted Christians

DISCOURAGEMENT-BUSTING QUESTIONS PERTAINING TO EXPERIENCES OF TROUBLE:

- From the perspective of my entire life, and even more

than that, eternity, how significant is my trouble?
- With God, is a good outcome impossible?
- Have others encountered a similar trouble and not only survived, but thrived?
- Every bad circumstance has good outcome options; what are mine?
- My trouble is not unique; what can I learn from others to help me?
- How can I use my trouble as a testimony to encourage others?
- As a disciple of Jesus, is my mistake, failure or sin unredeemable?

SCRIPTURE'S COUNSEL TO THE DISCOURAGED:
- Understand that God is sovereign
- Trust that God can work out all things for good
- Remember how God has already helped
- Believe that all troubles have meaning and purpose
- Live by faith, not by sight
- Worship
- Pray

OTHER TANGIBLE PRACTICES THAT DISPEL DISCOURAGEMENT:
- Save cards, notes and emails of appreciation or encouragement.
- Write down words of encouragement from others given verbally.
- Create lists of songs, books or movies that brighten the day.
- Get the mind on a different 'track' by serving someone else.
- Make a running blessing list.

Letter Thirty-Seven

- Send a "well done" or "thank you" note.
- Recall experiences that result in a smile or laugh.

I hope that list-making will provide you another option by which you may be empowered to dispel the discouragement that eventually strikes each of us in some form or another. As a disciple of Jesus, I invite you to share the lists with others to rally their spirit in times of discouragement. Such an exercise is a means of building the Body of Christ in the world of troubles.

> "Lists are a form of power."
> A.S. Byatt, British Poet & Author

Be blessed, my friends.

REFLECTIONS

LETTER THIRTY-EIGHT

My 'Stops and Starts'

RECLAIMING A POSITIVE AND HEALTHY DISCIPLESHIP POSTURE

"There is a time for everything,
and a season for every activity under heaven."
Proverbs 3:1

"You're always one choice away from changing your life."
A common maxim

Hello Friends.

I crack up every time I watch Bob Newhart's "Stop it!" Youtube video (I included a link in this article's footnotes)[68]. It is both amusing and illuminating. The basic plot is that as the counseling client shares her list of problem behaviours, Dr. Newhart repeatedly tells her to just *"Stop it!"* Stop doing the unhealthy behaviour. Beneath the hilarious quips is a degree of practical wise counsel many of us need. It draws a person like me into asking, *"What unhealthy personal practices do I need to just stop?"*

Speaking of therapy, although I am not a fan of the TV show *Dr. Phil*, I really like Dr. McGraw's repeated question when confronting people engaged in unhealthy behaviours: *"How's that working for you?"* How many of us need to be asked that very question about the practices in our own life? Full disclosure. I do. And yet, the question seems to be difficult to ask. The impediment seems to be that making such an inquiry means the very plausible need for a significant change. And, for many, such a life-change may be too daunting.

I have recently done a lot of reading on micro-changes or micro-habits. The basic premise here is that instead of making major changes in one's life to alter behaviour, a person could make a series of small (micro) changes. The argument is that little changes can result in big outcomes; small changes change everything. I really resonate with this line of thinking.

With the help of the Holy Spirit and the wisdom of Scripture, I am trying to put into practice a series of these behavioral micro-changes. I want to be a healthy and positive disciple of Jesus. The remainder of this article's space shares ten micro-changes I am striving to make – my *stops and starts*. Also noted are supplementary inspirational sentiments I have jotted down in my journal over the years. In the past these insightful postulations have served to rally my spirit toward change.[69]

1. STOP lamenting about what you don't have, START celebrating what you do have. *"You gotta look for the good in the bad, the happy in the sad, the gain in the pain, and what makes you grateful not hateful."* Karen Salmansohn
"You may have been given a cactus, but you don't have to sit on it." Joyce Meyer
2. STOP fixating upon those who are against you, START collaborating with those who are for you. *Focusing on your detractors – especially trying to appease them – is a recipe for a high degree of frustration and ultimately a failure in your mission.*
Naysayers don't make good team players.
3. STOP venturing down rabbit holes, START keeping the main thing the main thing. *"The main thing is to keep the main thing the main thing."* Stephen R. Covey
The disciples' 'main thing' is to live out the Great Commission and the Greatest Commandment.
4. STOP doubting that your experience has purpose, START believing God intends it for good. *Faith doesn't mean I know where I'm going; it means I'm trusting God with wherever He's leading me. God is still writing your story. Quit trying to steal the pen. Trust the writer.*

5. STOP acting like you can fix the problems of the season, START inviting God to redeem them. *"Pray and let God worry."* Martin Luther *"How completely satisfying to turn from our limitations to a God who has none."* A.W. Tozer
6. STOP focusing on what isn't working, START building upon what is. *"Insanity is doing the same thing over and over and expecting different results."* Albert Einstein *"The secret of change is to focus all of your energy not on fighting the old, but on building the new."* Socrates
7. STOP dying by a '1000 cuts,' START making necessary ones. *"You cannot thrive without pruning....Pruning is a process of proactive endings."* Henry Cloud *"For the right tomorrow to come, some parts of today may have to come to a necessary ending."* Henry Cloud
8. STOP unmeasured consumption of the doom and gloom on social media, START a routine robust diet of Scripture's hope and joy. *An entire sea of water cannot sink a ship unless it gets inside the ship. Similarly, the negativity of the world cannot pull you down unless you allow it to get inside you.* *"If I look to the world, I will conform to the ways of the world. If I look at the Word, I will conform to the will of God."* A.W. Tozer
9. STOP functioning like you have no limits, START operating within them. *"I'm sorry to be so brutally clear in making this point, but life is, in many ways, a zero – sum game...Admitting and accepting limits is a sign of maturity. Many of us never get this far. We keep entertaining the fiction that life is elastic, that we can stretch it like spandex...The uncompromising truth is that whenever our lives are full, they are full."* Richard A. Swenson

Letter Thirty-Eight

> "*What happens when overload collides with faith? Joy is an early casualty.*" Richard A. Swenson

10. STOP letting others set your priorities, START articulating your own. *If you don't set your calendar, there are many who will. I can only please one person per day. Today is not your day; tomorrow doesn't look good either.* N.J. Nielsen

As you endeavour to ask the tough questions about your own unhealthy personal practices, may the Holy Spirit and the wisdom of Scripture give you both insight and courage. Living life with stops and starts like those above can be both healthy and life-transforming. I would counsel you to start by engaging in a small number of your own small changes (two or three for example) and achieve victories here before moving on to others. Don't try the 'firehose' approach.

Let me close by sharing a story. With a huge grin on my face, I recall teaching my girlfriend (now wife) how to drive my Honda Civic, a standard. It was an experience. There were moments that I thought all her stops, starts, hops and jerks with my Civic would ruin its clutch. There were bouts of frustration, exasperation, and downright emotional explosions as she tried to master the combination of clutch, gas pedal, and shifter. However, she persisted and eventually mastered driving a standard. I too survived; thanks for asking. The same is true with the stops and starts I mention above. Here too will be bouts of frustration, exasperation, and emotional fireworks. My friends, persevere. Eventually, you'll be able to shift into your micro-changes smoothly.

Letters to my Friends

> *"Your life today is a result of your thinking yesterday.*
> *Your life tomorrow will be determined by what you do today."*
> John C. Maxwell

Be blessed, my friends.

Letter Thirty-Eight

REFLECTIONS

Letters to my Friends

LETTER THIRTY-NINE

Just One More

WHEN YOU'RE THINKING ABOUT GIVING UP.

"So we're not giving up."
2 Corinthians 4:16a MSG.

"Quitting never makes anything easier."
Admiral William H. McRaven, U.S. Navy Seals

Letters to my Friends

Hello Friends.

Growing up on the family farm in Clearbrook, B.C., a most despised chore during spring was collecting large rocks out of mom's huge garden. I am convinced that her garden produced an annual crop of sizeable stones for us Gunther boys to harvest before we planted the multitude of vegetable seeds on hand. Under mom's watchful eye, we plucked rock after rock, placing them in small metal pails and then carrying them to the tractor bucket at the edge of the garden where we off loaded our 'harvest.' It was mundane repetitive labour that never seemed to end. My mom sensed when we were on the verge of quitting and rallied us by saying, "Just one more pail. Just one more pail." In response, we kept on keeping on, rock after rock, pail after pail. Eventually, the seemingly impossible work (from a young boy's perspective) was completed, and the aches forgotten. The lesson mom taught me all those years ago in the garden was not lost on me. Today, when tasked with something seemingly impossible and I want to throw in the towel, I hear mom's voice telling me, "Just one more pail. Just one more pail."

The place was New Orleans, the date September 7, 1892, and the occasion a much-anticipated boxing match between an undefeated heavy weight champion John L. Sullivan, nicknamed the Boston Strong Boy, and a relatively unknown brawler named Gentlemen James John "Jim" Corbett. The fisticuff took place in front of 10,000 raucous spectators. The match went on round after round with each tough hard-hitting fighter landing powerful blows upon their opponent's body. Finally, in the 21st round Corbett landed a smashing left-hand hook to Sullivan's jaw and the bloody contest was over. Corbett's fighting style landed him the title Father of Modern Boxing. Corbett was later recorded as saying, "You become a champion by fighting one more round. When things are tough, you fight one more round."

> God does not give us overcoming life: He gives us life as we overcome. The strain is the strength.
> Oswald Chambers. Author, *My Utmost for His Highest*

In 2019, Nepali mountaineer Nirmal Nimsdair Purja began a quest he called *Project Possible*, the climbing of the world's fourteen 8000 metre plus mountain peaks in seven months. The only other alpinist to achieve climbing these fourteen peaks was Reinhold Messner and it took him sixteen years! Purja's quest included ascending mountains in Nepal, China, Pakistan and Tibet with names like Everest, K2, Nangaparbatt and Makalu. His adventure was recorded in the documentary *14 Peaks: Nothing Is Impossible*. Watching Purja in this film ascend these massive peaks was nothing short of stunning. He seemed to have the stamina of ten men and the determination of a hundred. His constant mantras included: "Giving up is not in the blood," and "Don't be afraid to dream big." Watching him face fierce winds, frigid temperatures, lack of oxygen, dizzying heights and grueling exhaustion was spellbinding. No matter what challenge he faced, he simply took one more step towards the summit, and then another, and another, and another, and eventually he rested at the peak. Purja accomplished a seemingly impossible feat.

"Noah was a righteous man, blameless among the people of his time and he walked with God" (Genesis 6:9b NIV). He was over 500 years old when the call of God came to him to build an ark of cypress wood 450 feet long, 75 feet wide and 45 feet high. This mammoth building project had a purpose; to save human and animal life from a catastrophic flood. Biblical commentators estimate the build took upwards of 75 years to complete. We are told little about the culture of the time other than "great wickedness" abounded. We can only speculate the response of Noah's community to his testimony that God had called him to build an ark in order to save human and animal life from a great flood. What would you think if someone told you that today? The amazing thing is that no matter what challenges Noah faced – scarce resources, opposition, doubt or fatigue – he fastened plank after plank on the frame of the ark until it was ready to carry life above the waters.

Stone by stone the wall of Jerusalem, destroyed by Nebuchadnezzar in 586 B.C., was being rebuilt under the capable godly leadership of Nehemiah. It was 446 B.C. and for 140 years the physical protection of the formerly exiled Jews was nothing but rubble. They were exposed and vulnerable to any and all who would plot to bring them harm. Their recently built temple was also susceptible to destruction by enemies. The citizens of Jerusalem felt disgraced and ashamed as they gazed upon the ruins of their stone bulwark. Nehemiah called this reconstruction "the great work," a resurrection of

Letter Thirty-Nine

tangible security ordained by God himself (Nehemiah 6:3,16). He rallied skilled and unskilled labourers, men, women, young and old in the face of foreign agitators, internal squabbles, and organizational complications. He had every reason not to continue and simply return to his comfortable day job in the Persian court under Artaxerxes. However, Nehemiah laid one more stone, and another, and another, eventually rebuilding the Jerusalem wall in 52 days.

> Every difficult task that comes across your path – every one that you would rather not do, that will take the most effort, cause the most pain, and be the greatest struggle – brings a blessing.
>
> L.B. Cowman
> Author, *Streams in the Desert*

One more pail. One more round. One more step. One more plank. One more stone. One more. As a disciple of Jesus, I am convinced that I will be called to remove 'rocks' so that something new can be sown. I will be called to fight battles – spiritual or otherwise – so that peace or justice can prevail. I will be called to ascend impossible 'massifs' to advance the gospel. I will be called to construct a means by which another might be saved from impending personal destruction. I will be called to rebuild and restore broken hopes so that joy can return. My prayer is that when the rocks seem endless, the body feels exhausted, the mountain screams "I'm unassailable," the project overwhelms me or the wall looks too broken, I will appeal to the Lord for strength to make just one more effort, spend one more day, give it one more attempt. I will remember the words of Paul to the churches in the province of Galatia: "Let us not become weary in doing good, for at the proper time we will reap a harvest if we do not give up" (Galatians 6:9).

> *"It always seems impossible until it's done."*
> Nelson Mandela

Be blessed, my friends.

Letter Thirty-Nine

REFLECTIONS

Letters to my Friends

LETTER FORTY

~~Just One More~~ One Too Many

WHEN GIVING UP IS THE BETTER CHOICE

"There's an opportune time to do things,
a right time for everything on the earth...
A right time to hold on and another to let go."
Ecclesiastes 3:1,6b MSG.

"Great is the art of the beginning,
but greater is the art of ending."
Henry Wadsworth Longfellow

Hello Friends.

It was a 1990 Mercury Sable, and it was a money pit. Every month, without fail, it was at the garage for repairs of some mechanical malady. It wasn't until the cost of fixing this beast equalled its purchase price that I finally decided enough was enough and sold the lemon. I made a necessary ending.

Years later, I enrolled in a doctorate program, excited about sharpening my ministry skills. The church I served gave me the resources and space to complete the degree. At the time I was working fulltime and raising three young children with my wife. After a year of study, I began to realize the negative impact my studies were having on my family. I was sacrificing time with my children and wife; time I could never recoup. My family needed me more than I needed another degree. I withdrew from the program.

> "Prudent is the one who gives thought to their steps."
> Proverbs 14:15b

Acknowledged to be the best hockey player in history, the "Great One" held 61 NHL records during his twenty-one years of play from 1978-1999. He won nine most valuable player trophies, five outstanding player of the year trophies and ten trophies for most points in a season. He scored a total of 894 goals and racked up 1963 assists during his hockey career. At the age of 38, to the stunned surprise of the NHL and his fans, Wayne Gretzky gave up his skates. It was said that he hoped to leave the fans

Letter Forty

wanting more rather than wishing for less. Many felt he quit too early; that he had so much more to offer the game and his fans. Gretzky stated that he had a gut feeling it was time: "It's hard. This is a great game, but it's a hard game. I'm ready."[70] His reoccurring back injuries, a sense that there was nothing of significance for him to accomplish record-wise, and a desire to spend more time with his family, were given as reasons for quitting one career and starting another. This new path included coaching, hockey team ownership and pursuing various business ventures. Gretzky believed retirement from hockey was a necessary ending.

Consider the following narrative in the life of Jesus:

> "One day Jesus called together his twelve disciples and gave them power and authority to cast out all demons and to heal all diseases. Then he sent them out to tell everyone about the Kingdom of God and to heal the sick. "Take nothing for your journey," he instructed them. "Don't take a walking stick, a traveler's bag, food, money, or even a change of clothes. Wherever you go, stay in the same house until you leave town. And if a town refuses to welcome you, shake its dust from your feet as you leave to show that you have abandoned those people to their fate"
> (Luke 9:1-5 NLT).

Here Jesus called for a necessary ending to a specific ministry for a specific time and situation despite the people's desperate need to hear about, and respond to, the Kingdom of God that was unfolding before them. If they did not want to hear this good news, the disciples were to walk away, *"abandoning"* them to their fate. Sometimes even Jesus himself knew that there was a time to quit and move on and he directed his followers to do so. There was a time for a necessary ending.

My parents instilled in me the conviction to never, ever give up on anything. Like me, many of my generation were raised on the adage that *"quitters never win."* I am truly thankful my parent's coaching me; reminding me to stay the course, to hold the line, to never walk away. However, my life experiences have taught me that sometimes the best decision is, in fact, to bring something to an end. I have personally walked with colleagues who could not bring something to close that needed to end. Their relationships, health and ministry suffered as a result. In his work, *Necessary Endings*, Dr. Henry Cloud speaks to this matter of never giving up, no matter the cost:

> "...there is a toxic version of not quitting. It happens when the label of "quitting" in the big sense is equated with stopping a particular goal or endeavour. In other words, if you quit any one thing, you are a quitter instead of being wise... Quitting is just bad, period. Always, anytime, anywhere.
>
> Furthermore, the label gets attached not to the project or the individual case, but the self. "I am a quitter," is what goes through the person's head, instead of "I decided to fold on this particular hand. It was stupid to go forward" ...some people have maps in their heads that say, "Any giving up is bad." This belief keeps them from endings that should happen...Sometimes it makes sense to quit a particular project or goal. It does not mean you are a "quitter."[71]

Letter Forty

Cloud's insightful perspective is wise and genuinely helpful. A decision on whether to keep on with something or to end it requires a healthy portion of perspective, self-awareness, grace and on-going reality checks. I am the wiser when I consider my options carefully and when I bathe all of these personal 'safety-checks' in prayer, the counsel of Scripture and the wisdom of godly believers.

> Sometimes the best way is a different way.
> Anonymous

As followers of Jesus, we should not easily walk away from our commitment to significant goals, projects, or work. I have determined that although there are elements of the labour that might cause me to think about giving up, I will not quit because the work

- is great or long;
- requires some sacrifice;
- runs into trouble or has opponents;
- raises doubts or brings confusion;
- requires a personal life-change; or
- requires realignment or retooling.

We all have pursued something, at all costs, and discovered it has only reaped heartache and heartbreak. The negative consequences of a *"never give up"* approach may impact us even today – spiritually, mentally, physically, relationally. I still hold to the view that one should keep on keeping on regarding matters of significance, but my conviction about 'giving up' has matured and become less rigid. Today, I test the degree of my pursuit of significant matters – even when it is something I believe God has called me to – by asking several questions:

- Is it in harmony with God's purposes, Scripture, and the counsel of godly peers?
- Is the Holy Spirit affirming me to continue?
- Is it enhancing my Christlikeness?
- Is it moving me to abide with Jesus?
- Is it life-giving?
- Is it causing harm to myself or others?
- What role is personal pride playing here?

I acknowledge these questions are deeply intertwined, but there is a depth of certainty, a heightened clarity, by engaging them all.

At the end of the day, sticking with something through thick and thin has a long list of commendable character-building outcomes. Resolve, self-control, loyalty, resilience, selflessness and courage are all enhanced by staying the course. However, there is an equal enhancement of personal character when making a necessary ending. May the Holy Spirit guide us all in these matters.

"...for the right tomorrow to come, some parts of today may have to come to a necessary ending."
Dr. Henry Cloud

Be blessed, my friends.

Letter Forty

REFLECTIONS

Letters to my Friends

LETTER FORTY-ONE

Good News People in Bad News Times

IF THE CHURCH DOES NOT PROCLAIM THE HOPE OF CHRIST, THEN WHO WILL?

> "But my life is worth nothing to me unless I use it for
> finishing the work assigned me by the Lord Jesus—
> the work of telling others the Good News
> about the wonderful grace of God."
> Acts 20:24

> "Out in the highways and byways of life,
> many are weary and sad.
> Carry the sunshine where darkness is rife,
> making the sorrowing glad.
> Make me a blessing,
> make me a blessing,
> out of my life may Jesus shine.
> Make me a blessing, O Savior, I pray,
> make me a blessing to someone today."[72]
> Ira B. Wilson, 1924

Hello Friends.

You may not believe this, but there is a secular social media platform dedicated solely to communicating GOOD NEWS. The *GoodNewsNetwork.org* is promoted as being "an antidote to the barrage of negativity experienced in the mainstream media...it is a daily dose of hope."[73] My favorite stories so far have been: "Stray Cats Saved A Restaurant During The Pandemic" and "Banjo Player Serenades A Fox In Colorado." I know that right now you are smiling, and maybe even making fun of these headlines, but you're SMILING and having FUN! Friends, we desperately need and long for things that will brighten our lives, make us smile, laugh, and celebrate. Amen? Amen, indeed.

The *Canadian Medical Association Journal* posted an article stating that people are consuming a rapidly increasing diet of negative news. This practice, the journal claims, is contributing to a worsening of mental health. Many people, asserts Dr. Cecille Ahrens, are stuck in a pattern of frequently monitoring bad news which in turn leads to elevated moodiness and anxiety. This harmful and habitual pattern of behaviour has been dubbed '*doomscrolling.*'[74] Doomscrolling is "the act of obsessively reading bad news despite the onset of anxiety."[75] Distress and depression are a common outcome of doomscrolling. Dr. Graham C.L. Davey writes in *Psychology Today* that the constant consumption of negative, and often sensationalized bad news, continues to cause significant unhealthy mood changes. Most notably, it fuels an individual's own personal worries.[76] The prolonged unhealthy intake of large quantities of bad news also exacerbates the symptoms and impact of serious physical ailments like arthritis, diabetes and cardiovascular disease.[77] In sum, an unhealthy diet of bad news is detrimental for mental and physical health. And yet, the world's consumption of bad and sad news shows no signs of abating. It is no wonder that the emotional and mental well-being of our communities in this country is collapsing at an alarming rate. People are 'bloated' with dark messaging. They are exhausted from searching, and not finding, a personal peace, joy or hope for a better future.

I am reminded of an Old Testament story about people in exactly in the same space. Some 850 years before the birth of Christ: "…Ben-Hadad king of Aram mobilized his entire army and marched up and laid siege to Samaria. There was a great famine in the city; the siege lasted so long that a donkey's head sold for eighty shekels [2 lbs.] of silver, and a quarter of a cab [1/2 pint] of seed pods for five shekels [2 lbs. of silver.]" (2 Kings 6:24-25). The starvation in the city was so horrific that cannibalism took place. On the throne of the besieged city was King Jehoram. Jehoram is so distraught about all the bad news he is encountering that he tears his robes in utter despair! In anger, Jehoram pronounces, "This disaster is from the Lord! (2 Kings 6:33)." Hearing about Jehoram's lament, God's prophet Elisha prophecies that the famine will be lifted – a prophecy of good news. The story continues…

> "Now there were four men with leprosy at the entrance of the city gate. They said to each other, "Why stay here until we die? If we say, 'We'll go into the city'—the famine is there, and

we will die. And if we stay here, we will die. So let's go over to the camp of the Arameans and surrender. If they spare us, we live; if they kill us, then we die." At dusk they got up and went to the camp of the Arameans. When they reached the edge of the camp, not a man was there, for the Lord had caused the Arameans to hear the sound of chariots and horses and a great army, so that they said to one another, "Look, the king of Israel has hired the Hittite and Egyptian kings to attack us!" So they got up and fled in the dusk and abandoned their tents and their horses and donkeys. They left the camp as it was and ran for their lives. The men who had leprosy reached the edge of the camp and entered one of the tents. They ate and drank, and carried away silver, gold and clothes, and went off and hid them. They returned and entered another tent and took some things from it and hid them also. Then they said to each other, "We're not doing right. *This is a day of good news* and we are keeping it to ourselves. If we wait until daylight, punishment will overtake us. *Let's go at once and report this* to the royal palace." So they went and called out to the city gatekeepers and told them, "We went into the Aramean camp and not a man was there—not a sound of anyone—only tethered horses and donkeys, and the tents left just as they were." The gatekeepers shouted the [good] news, and it was reported within the palace"
(2 Kings 7:3-11).

These four lepers were good news people in bad news times. Today, we as disciples of Jesus are to be good news people in bad news times, not with stories of stray cats or Colorado foxes or even a 'chicken soup'-like feel good testimony, but with life-transforming news that brings hope, peace and joy to the present and future. And friends, we can bear witness of such a thing:

> "And there were shepherds living out in the fields nearby, keeping watch over their flocks at night. An angel of the Lord appeared to them, and the glory of the Lord shone around them, and they were terrified. But the angel said to them, "Do not be afraid. *I bring you good news* that will cause great joy for all the people. Today in the town of David a Savior has been born to you; he is the Messiah, the Lord" (Luke 2:8-11).

> "Let me now remind you, dear brothers and sisters, of the Good News I preached to you before. You welcomed it then, and you still stand firm in it. *It is this Good News that saves you* if you continue to believe the message I told you—unless, of course, you believed something that was never true in the first place. I passed on to you what was most important and what had also been passed on to me. Christ died for our sins, just as the Scriptures said. He was buried, and he was raised from the dead on the third day, just as the Scriptures said" (2 Corinthians 15:1-4 NLT).

> "If you openly declare that Jesus is Lord and believe in your heart that God raised him from the dead, you will be saved. For it is by believing in your heart that you are made right with God, and it is by openly declaring your faith that you are saved....But how can they call on him to save them unless they believe in him? And how can they believe in him if they have never heard about him? And how can they hear about him unless someone tells them? And how will anyone go and

tell them without being sent? That is why the Scriptures say, *"How beautiful are the feet of messengers who bring good news!"* (Romans 10:8b-15 NLT).

Reality check. We cannot genuinely bring this good news until our heart truly knows it. Both require the ministry of the Holy Spirit. To be good news bearers and bringers, we must first be supernaturally redeemed by Christ – "born again" (John 3:16), made into a "new creation" (2 Corinthians 5:17), possessing minds and eyes fixed on Jesus (Hebrews 3:1; 12:2). From this space, our opportunity in the present bad and sad news culture is boundless and plentiful.

Today, are you a good news bearer and bringer? In the spirit of Psalm 139:23-24, ask God to search your heart as you make the following personal inquiries:

- Does my heart reflect a good news posture?
- Does my thinking reflect a good news perspective?
- Do my words reflect a good news spirit?
- Do my actions reflect a good news motivation?

May the community in which we live say about us as disciples of Jesus: "How beautiful are the feet of those who bring good news!"

Be blessed, my friends.

Letter Forty-One

REFLECTIONS

Letters to my Friends

LETTER FORTY-TWO
Sabbath

Hello Friends.

Pilgrims was written on July 14, 2014, while on a spiritual retreat in Ladysmith, British Columbia. It was wordsmithed on April 14, 2022. I was moved to write this work after contemplating the words of the Welsh pastor and biblical scholar Matthew Henry who wrote, "This world is our passage and not our portion."

PILGRAMS

> We are pilgrims passing through,
>> travelers purposed for a quest.
>
> We are spiritual beings on an earthly passage,
>> souls plodding along a material way.
>
> This life is a blessing, a gift of great worth,
>> but brief, a wisp, a vapor, a breath.
>
> Like lilies we bloom but a season and then fold,
>> like billowing clouds, we are soon whisked away.
>
> Like sand in an hourglass, eventually we fall,
>> like the sea's tide, we all go out.
>
> From dust our frame rose, to dust it returns,
>> but our soul carries on.
>
> In this moment set your hearts on pilgrimage,
>> your eyes on a sacred path.
>
> Seek him who made us eternal,
>> him who fashioned us everlasting.
>
> We are pilgrims passing through,
>> travelers purposed for a quest.

Letter Forty-Two

SABBATH PRAYER

A Prayer to Center my Heart was first put to paper on January 9, 2012, in Regina, Saskatchewan.

"From inside the fish Jonah prayed to the LORD his God."
Jonah 2:1

"My secret is a very simple one: I pray."
Mother Teresa

A PRAYER TO CENTER MY HEART

>Freely, in the stillness of this space, I open
>   my soul to you, O God.
>Holy Spirit, I welcome you; guide me in this
>   moment.
>Guard my heart and mind from the evil one.
>Demolish the inner walls I have constructed
>   against doing what pleases you.
>Cast out any fear and all doubt that may
>   impede the surrender of my heart.
>Empower me to set aside my fleshly biases.
>Prepare my spirit, O God, so that I might be
>   fully present and available.
>Help me release those temporary things that
>   have consumed my thoughts.
>Lord, grant me discernment to distill what
>   I hear, wisdom to respond rightly.
>Calm my soul, compose my mind, focus the
>   eyes of my heart upon you.

Letters to my Friends

Bless me with courage to forge my will into harmony with what you reveal.
O God, I am an untouched canvas awaiting your revelation, an empty scroll anticipating your words.
Amen.

Heartwork II – Grace Like Rain, PG, 2012.

Letter Forty-Two

REFLECTIONS

Letters to my Friends

WEEK VII

LETTER FORTY-THREE

Chasing Joy (Part One)

THE PASSIONATE AND PUZZLING PURSUIT

"You have made known to me the paths of life;
you will fill me with your joy in your presence."
Acts 2:28

"A Christian should be an Alleluia from head to foot."
St. Augustine of Hippo

Hello Friends.

We all need a greater portion of joy in our lives; I know I do. Joy is that intangible, yet tangible, treasure that all of us long for but few discover in any lasting or substantial quantity. Joy, like physical health, is important to most of us. We speak of it often, most times expressing a longing for it. In this, and three additional subsequent letters, I share my quest for a better understanding of joy. My sincere hope is that as you read my reflections and sentiments you will encounter the joy that you need for your time and space. Not all that long ago, a colleague shared that his devotional focus for the year was "Chasing Joy." Instantly intrigued, I began a quest and soon discovered that the constitution of this thing we call "joy" is both self-evident and a mystery. The inextricable aspects of joy were notable and caught me unawares. In his article, *The Power of Joy*, Jeffrey Kluger wrote, "Defining joy is a fool's gambit – like trying to parse a joke or diagram love or lift a sand sculpture. To examine it is to have it run through your fingers."[78] Kluger's sentiments challenge me. To be honest though, I'm beginning to sense that the 'chasing' part of "Chasing Joy" is an apt descriptor.

There are several things known about joy. It is visceral, an emotion, a robust cheerfulness of the spirit. It is without question an experience passionately sought after, but hard to come by. It is a kindred spirit to happiness, and yet different: "Happiness is an inch deep and a mile wide, whereas joy is a mile deep and a mile wide."[79] Unlike happiness, joy appears less anchored to one's circumstances. According to C.S. Lewis, the only thing happiness has in common with joy is that those who experience it, long for it again. I am well aware, personally, that joy is experienced by people of all cultures and creeds and in the midst of all circumstances. Of note is that people of faith in God know it with greater consistency and intensity. Joy and the intimate moving of God in one's life are supernaturally interwoven.[80] Our human genome has a tiny bit to do with how we experience joy, but our mindset, relationship with others (and God), and the depth of our gratitude, is of far greater relevance. Joy is equally inexplicable. I penned the following in my personal journal about the challenge of grasping joy's meaning:

> "Joy is an amazing thing. All of us know it by touch, but none of us can honestly claim to be able to fully articulate what it truly means. Explaining joy is not simple, it is multi-layered; a gift to be revealed and something to be sought. It is found in celebration and in hardship. It is found in the souls of others and in the heart of God. It is not happiness, but one would be hard-pressed to delineate between the two. It is embedded in hope, peace and love, but stands wholly apart from them as well. It is able to render tears and dancing in the same moment. It is both subtle and effusive, resilient and fragile. The longer its constitution is explored, the greater its illusive nature is revealed. Joy is a mystery of the divine that our soul craves and pursues."[81]

Humankind has longed to capture the essence of joy and pondered ways to speak of it. In 1785 German poet Friedrich Schiller's *Ode to Joy* was a popular attempt.

Schiller's poem spoke of joy as being the "spark of divinity." In 1824 Ludwig van Beethoven enveloped it in the music of his Ninth Symphony. In 1907 Henry van Dyck married Beethoven's music to the worship lyrics *Joyful, Joyful, We Adore Thee*. In another corner of the world ancient Egyptians believed the gods would ask them two questions as a test for entry into the Field of Reeds (paradise), "Did you bring joy?" and "Did you find joy"? The Catholic church includes joy in the first bead chaplet of their prayer rosary known as the Five Joyful Mysteries (of Christ).

Over the centuries a plethora of songs, books and movies have interpreted joy for our consideration; each artistic expression carrying a unique view to how it blossoms in life. In business, the word "joy" is often used to vend products (eg. *Almond Joy* chocolate bars, the *Joy of Cooking* cookbook, *Ultra Joy* dishwashing soap). In addition, there is no shortage of joy focused self-help books to cure what ails you. And yet, after umpteen years of elucidation, the 'soul' of joy remains ever illusive.

So, if joy is difficult to pin down, hard to grasp, and not easy to find and maintain, what is a helpful and fruitful way forward as disciples of Christ? Perhaps a beginning point is acknowledging the relationship between joy and God's work in our lives.

In the next letter, I share my thoughts about the ultimate source of joy.

Be blessed, my friends.

Letter Forty-Three

REFLECTIONS

Letters to my Friends

LETTER FORTY-FOUR

Chasing Joy (Part Two)

THE PASSIONATE AND PUZZLING PURSUIT

"Do not grieve, for the joy of the Lord is your strength."
Nehemiah 8:10c

"Joy is strength."
Mother Teresa

Hello Friends.

The French priest, theologian and philosopher, Pierre Teilhard de Chardin, penned, "Joy is the infallible sign of the presence of God."[82] C.S. Lewis claimed that the ultimate source of his joy was also God; joy was a signpost to him through Christ Jesus. He once wrote, "Joy is the serious business of heaven."[83] In my own pilgrimage through life, I have observed those who genuinely walk with God not only experience great abiding joy, but they are also a conduit for it. As children, how many of us sang the words "Joy is the flag flown high from the castle of my heart...when the King (God/Jesus) is in residence there"? At Christmas we jubilantly give voice to the words "Joy to the world the Lord has come! Let earth receive her King!"

God is the creator (source) of all things, including joy (Psalm 146:6; John 1:3; Ephesians 3:9). Scripture proffers much about the connection between God and joy: "There I will go to the altar of God, to God the source of my joy" (Psalm 43:4); "The joy of the Lord is my strength" (Nehemiah 8:10); "God, my joy and delight" (Psalm 43:4). Furthermore, the kingdom of God is a "matter of righteousness, peace and joy" (Romans 14:17); the fruit of the Holy Spirit is joy (Galatians 5:22) and with the Lord, our joy is complete (1 John 1:1-4). Joy's origin is divine.

As a young adult in my home church, I can still recall singing the joy-saturated song *Therefore the redeemed of the Lord*. For me the song celebrated my own redemption through the person and work of Christ.

"Therefore the redeemed of the
Lord shall return,
And come with singing unto Zion;
And everlasting joy shall be upon
their head. (repeat)
They shall obtain gladness and joy;
And sorrow and mourning shall flee
away."

The person and work of Christ brings new life – eternal life – the salvation of our souls. Simply put, Christ brings joy. Rather than adding too much of my own commentary, Scripture can speak for itself.

> "Praise be to the God and Father of our Lord Jesus Christ! In his great mercy he has given us new birth into a living hope through the resurrection of Jesus Christ from the dead, and into an inheritance that can never perish, spoil or fade. This inheritance is kept in heaven for you, who through faith are shielded by God's power until the coming of the salvation that is ready to be revealed in the last time. In all this you greatly rejoice, though now for a little while you may have had to suffer grief in all kinds of trials. These have come so that the proven genuineness of your faith–of greater worth than gold, which perishes even though refined by fire–may result in praise, glory and honor when Jesus Christ is revealed. Though you have not seen him, you love him; and even though you do not see him now, you believe in him and are filled with an inexpressible and glorious joy, for you are receiving the end result of your faith, the salvation of your souls." 1 Peter 1:3-9

The word rejoice here means a deep spiritual joy. Carol McLeod, author of *Vibrant* provides some insightful commentary: "The ability to greatly rejoice does not come from your personality, your circumstances, or from what is visible. It comes from the deep assurance that God loves us and that He will write the end of our stories well...Joy is not the absence of troubles, but the presence of Christ."[84] What an amazing encouragement!

In the next letter, I will share my thoughts about the connection between joy and serving others.

Be blessed, my friends.

Letter Forty-Four

REFLECTIONS

Letters to my Friends

LETTER FORTY-FIVE

Chasing Joy (Part Three)

THE PASSIONATE AND PUZZLING PURSUIT

"And the angel said unto them, Fear not, for behold,
I bring you good tidings of great joy
which shall be to all people."
Luke 2:10 KJV

"Joy overflows."
Mother Teresa

Hello Friends.

American basketball player, coach, and author John Wooden once said, "Helping others is perhaps the greatest joy."[85] In my early discipleship, the acronym J.O.Y. was impressed upon me. It stood for "Jesus, others, you" implying that as disciples of Jesus, we put Him first, others second and ourselves last. Core to experiencing joy was loving and serving others; it was second only to Jesus. In pastoral ministry I learned that the most joyless people were those whose life was focused on themselves. In fact, these folks were like black holes that sucked joy from the room. Conversely, when one's mindset is on seeking the best interests of another, joy is present. Not only does one experience joy in serving others, when one is full of joy, serving others seems to be a natural outcome. Mother Teresa wrote, "When you are full of joy…you want to go about doing good to everyone."[86] Joy comes from serving, and joyful people serve.

Scripture is helpful in expanding our knowledge regarding those who are joyful. For example, "Joyful is the person who finds wisdom" (Proverbs 3:13), "Joyful are those who trust in the Lord" (Proverbs 16:20), "Joyful are people of integrity" (Psalm 119:1), "How joyful are those who fear the Lord" (Psalm 112:1), and joyful are "those who deal justly with others and always do what is right" (Psalm 106:3). Writing about these must be left for another time, but I will comment that the joy spoken of here implies a chasing. In this vein, Henri J.M. Nouwen wrote, "Joy does not simply happen to us. We have to choose joy and keep choosing it every day."[87] By our actions we indirectly either choose or bypass a slice of joy.

Swiss theologian Karl Barth claimed that joy is the simplest form of gratitude. Gratitude bears the fruit of joy. Gratitude is certainly Scripture's counsel: "Always be thankful" (Colossians 3:15); "Be thankful in all circumstances, for this is God's will for you who belong to Christ Jesus" (1 Thessalonians 5:18). There is wisdom behind this inspired word, and I know from practice that when I pause to recollect the blessings in my life, I become thankful and joyful. Although I cannot find a biblical passage directly stating joy comes from a grateful heart, Psalm 100, the go-to text on Thanksgiving Day, points to a relationship:

> "Shout with joy to the Lord, all the earth!
> Worship the Lord with gladness.
> Come before him, singing with joy.
> Acknowledge that the Lord is God!
> He made us, and we are his.
> We are his people, the sheep of his pasture.
> Enter his gates with thanksgiving;
> go into his courts with praise.
> Give thanks to him and praise his name.
> For the Lord is good.
> His unfailing love continues forever,
> and his faithfulness continues to each generation"
> (Psalm 100 NLT).

In the next letter, I will share my thoughts about the connection between joy and suffering.

Be blessed, my friends.

REFLECTIONS

LETTER FORTY-SIX

Chasing Joy (Part Four)

THE PASSIONATE AND PUZZLING PURSUIT

"When anxiety was great within me,
your consolation brought me joy."
Psalm 94:19

"Think joy, talk joy, share joy."
Norman Vincent Peale

Hello Friends.

The collective personal anecdotes I could share about where joy is *not* found could fill a thousand pages but let me simply submit that in my experience genuine joy has never been found in fame, fortune, power or positive psychology. They may offer a fleeting form of happiness, but not abiding joy. In fact, too often they come with debilitating disillusionment. And, what of choosing life without God? The truth is that every person on earth experiences joy in some fashion, but to what degree is joy forfeited when God is rejected or ignored? I surmise that walking away from the divine source of joy would bring despair much like leaving a campfire would result in feeling cold.

I am convinced that the disciple who possesses a deep reservoir of joy once stood in a dark well of despair. There is something about suffering that creates the opportunity for joy to take root and flourish in the soul. When I think about those in my life that exhibit an abiding joy, all of them have walked in hurt, hardship, heartbreak. My life experiences have taught me that one cannot truly know deep joy unless one knows profound gloom or know peace without conflict or rest without weariness. The early Apostles knew this deep joy, in part, because they experienced persecution and trials. I recall Paul and Silas in the Philippian jail praying and singing hymns (Acts 16:25). They lived out of their joy, even while chained.

Scripture instructs disciples to not flee hardship because of their faith in Christ, but rather to embrace it for the fruit it will produce in their life:

> "Consider it pure joy, my brothers and sisters, whenever you face trials of many kinds, because you know that the testing of your faith produces perseverance. Let perseverance finish its work so that you may be mature and complete, not lacking anything"
> (James 1:2-4).

It is hard to imagine being joyful in our adversities, but that is Scripture's invitation. The Anabaptists understood persecution under the cross as a sign of the true church (true discipleship), and even as a form of 'blessing,' believing that the joy of their salvation in Christ would sustain them. Menno Simons spoke of every true disciple experiencing the "winepress of sorrow" for the sake of the cross, but in the end reaping joy as the King would express his delight in their sacrifice.[88] The psalmist entwines joy and suffering by writing: "...weeping may endure for a night, but joy cometh in the morning" (Psalm 30:5).

I would love to write about joy arising out of our identity and purpose in Christ or how a mindset of fixing our thoughts on heaven impacts experiencing joy, or even how physical and mental health intersects with the degree of joy one encounters in life. Reluctantly, this must be left for another time. The journey of pondering and writing about joy has been a blessing but I must now attend to other matters.

Friends, my best discernment on the matter of joy leads me to conclude that "chasing joy" is actually pursuing or receiving those things that bless us with it: God, the work of Christ, our identify as the beloved of

God, serving others, a grateful mindset, a godly lifestyle, wisdom and even physical and mental health. Equally, "chasing joy" is not courting sin, fame, fortune, power or positive psychology. All said and done, "chasing joy" is very much a life-long endeavour. In that light, I think John Wooden has the final apropos word, "Joy makes the longest journey too short."[89]

For today, just be encouraged to know that joy is within your reach.

Be blessed, my friends.

Letter Forty-Six

REFLECTIONS

Letters to my Friends

LETTER FORTY-SEVEN

Your 'Dash'

**WHAT WE DO IN LIFE ECHOES TO ETERNITY
(MAXIMUS)**

"What is your life? You are a mist that appears
for a little while and then vanishes."
James 4:14

"We are all mortal."
John F. Kennedy

Hello Friends.

Growing up I attended Simpson Elementary School in Clearbrook, B.C. Ray and I were the school's go-to guys for the 100-yard-dash race at the annual inter-school track meet. I did okay, but Ray usually edged me out. Ray has been my best friend since grade one – fifty-four years and counting. He still can beat me in any kind of dash. Seriously though, I want to share some thoughts on another kind of dash.

At a funeral, you are given obituary cards. These cards provide you with the deceased's date of birth and the date of their death. Between these two dates, what is usually found? A dash. It is also found on tombstones. Have you ever paused and reflected upon that small dash marking the time between birth and death? This small punctuation mark symbolizes a person's entire life, all that the deceased thought, said and did; all their relationships, accomplishments, failures and victories, fears, hopes and dreams.

The Bible describes our 'dash' several ways: "What is your life? You are a mist that appears for a little while and then vanishes" (James 4:14). "Our days on earth are like grass; like wildflowers, we bloom and die" (Psalm 90:15 NLT). "O Lord, what are human beings that you should notice them, mere mortals that you should think about them? For they are like a breath of air; their days are like a passing shadow" (Psalm 144:3,4 NLT).

Here's my observation: Our 'dash' is short and what we do with it is incredibly important. On either end of our 'dash' are dates. There is nothing you can do about the first date, your birth. This is out of your control. And, there is really very little you can control around the other end of your 'dash,' your death. The only thing you have some ability to shape is your 'dash'!

Allow me to share some biblical counsel to help you shape your 'dash':

YOUR 'DASH' IS A GIFT FROM THE CREATOR. NOTE THE FOLLOWING REVELATION FROM SCRIPTURE:

"So God created mankind in his own image, in the image of God he created them; male and female he created them" (Genesis 1:27).

"For you created my inmost being; you knit me together in my mother's womb. I praise you because I am fearfully and wonderfully made; your works are wonderful, I know that full well. My frame was not hidden from you when I was made in the secret place, when I was woven together in the depths of the earth" (Psalm 139:13-14).

The Apostle Paul said to the philosophers of Athens, "In [God] we live and move and have our being. As some of your poets have said, 'We are his offspring'" (Acts 17:25).

God "gives life to everything" (1 Timothy 6:13).

My counsel? Give thanks to God for the gift of your 'dash.'

YOUR 'DASH' HAS A PURPOSE. AGAIN, NOTE THE FOLLOWING REVELATION FROM SCRIPTURE:

"Know that the Lord is God. It is he who made us, and we are his; we are his people, the sheep of his pasture. Enter his gates with thanksgiving and his courts with praise; give thanks to him and praise his name" (Psalm 100:3,4).

"You are worthy, our Lord and God, to receive glory and honor and power, for you created all things, and by your will they were created and have their being" (Revelation 4:11).

In addition, Rick Warren, author of *The Purpose Driven Life*, wrote, "God did not need to create you, but He chose to create you for His own enjoyment. You exist for His benefit, His glory, His purpose, and His delight."[90]

The 1646 Westminster Catechism of the Church of England reads: "Man's chief end is to glorify [God] and enjoy him forever."

My counsel? Use your 'dash' to give God the worship he is due.

ULTIMATELY, THE LENGTH OF YOUR 'DASH' IS IN YOUR CREATOR'S HANDS. SCRIPTURE TEACHES:

"Man's days are determined; you have decreed the number of his months and have set limits he cannot exceed" (Job 14:5).

"All the days ordained for me were written in your book before one of them came to be" (Psalm 139:16b).

"Now listen, you who say, '"Today or tomorrow we will go to this or that city, spend a year there, carry on business and make money."' Why, you do not even know what will happen tomorrow. What is your life? You are a mist that appears for a little while and then vanishes. Instead, you ought to say, '"If it is the Lord's will, we will live and do this or that"' (James 4:13-15).

My counsel? Use the time you have in your 'dash' knowing its length is out of your hands.

YOUR 'DASH' IS NOT ALL THERE IS. IN THE OLD TESTAMENT WE READ:

"[God] has…set eternity in the hearts of men" (Ecclesiastes 3:11b). The writer of Ecclesiastes was referring to our soul; that part of us that sets us apart from all other living things – that part of us created in the image of God: "…Lord God formed man of the dust of the ground, and breathed into his nostrils the breath of life; and man became a living soul" (Genesis 2:7 KJV).

Our soul lives on after death. Atheists claim there is only your 'dash' and nothing more; we are not creations with eternal souls, but accidental evolved animals with expiry dates. If they had a theme song it would probably be the old classic song *Dust In The Wind* by the band Kansas.

> *"All we are is dust in the wind*
> *Dust in the wind*
> *Everything is dust in the wind."*

This is truly depressing! For those of us that believe we are eternal beings and that there is life after the 'dash,' here is some insight – live your 'dash' knowing there is life beyond it.

1. What you decide about your Creator during your 'dash' echoes to eternity.

The Scriptures teach this very thing when they call us to either decide for or against our Creator and his purposes. We see a revelation of his purposes in the words of His Son, Jesus: "Very truly I tell you, whoever hears my word and believes him who sent me has eternal life and will not be judged but has crossed over from death to life" (John 5:24). Again, Warren writes, "This life is preparation for the next."[91]

2. No matter what you do with your 'dash' one day you will have to give account for it to your Creator.

In the movie *Gladiator* Maximus is about to take his Roman troops into battle against the Germanic hordes. In rallying his fellow soldiers Maximus cries out, "What we do in life echoes to eternity!" Scripture teaches us: "So then, each of us will give an account of ourselves to God" (Romans 14:12). "Nothing in all creation is hidden from God's sight. Everything is uncovered and laid bare before the eyes of him to whom we must give account" (Hebrews 4:13).

Our sins echo into eternity; there they will either condemn us to life apart from God (for God cannot be

Letter Forty-Seven

in the presence of sin) or they will be set aside because of our faith in Christ Jesus and his sacrifice on the cross.

All of us have driven on a highway. We have seen the white or yellow center lines that divide the road. They are really dashes, aren't they? They certainly fly by at 100 kms per hour. As I read from Scripture earlier, our lives fly by as quickly. Each of us has precious little time in our 'dash.' What are you doing with it today? Are you living fully the gift of your 'dash'? Are you living your 'dash' knowing that you will have to one day give account for it to your Creator? Are you making those decisions that will carry you into life with God after your 'dash' is done?

We are all given a 'dash;' may God give us wisdom to live it in a way that is pleasing to him.

Be blessed, my friends.

Letters to my Friends

REFLECTIONS

Letter Forty-Eight

LETTER FORTY-EIGHT

All Things in Good Measure.

ABOUT LOOKING BACK

"Keep your eyes on Jesus..."
Hebrews 12:2, TLB

"Don't look back
A new day is break'in
It's been too long since I felt this way."
Boston, 1978, *Don't Look Back*

Letters to my Friends

Hello Friends.

I am somewhat of a history buff. Recently, I read a story that motivated me to some deeper pondering.

> "On August 7, 1954 during the British Empire and Commonwealth Games in Vancouver, B.C., England's Roger Bannister and Australian John Landy met for the first time in the one mile run at the newly constructed Empire Stadium.
>
> Both men had broken the four minute barrier previously that year. Bannister was the first to break the mark with a time of 3:59.4 on May 6th in Oxford England. Subsequently, on June 21st in Turku, Finland, John Landy became the new record holder with an official time of 3:58.
>
> The world watched eagerly as both men approached the starting blocks. As 35,000 enthusiastic fans looked on, no one knew what would take place on that historic day.
>
> Promoted as "The Mile of the Century," it would later be known as the "Miracle Mile."
>
> With only 90 yards to go in one of the world's most memorable races, John Landy glanced over his left shoulder to check his opponent's position. At that instant Bannister streaked by him to victory in a Commonwealth record time of 3:58.8."[92]

For days I 'chewed' on this story in my mind. The piece that bounced about in my thinking was how a

Letter Forty-Eight

simple act of looking back could be seemingly so instrumental in the course of one's life. Landy looked over his shoulder and at that moment Bannister passed him and went on to victory. In an interview after the race Landy stated that his looking back was not the reason he lost. Bannister, he confessed, was just a better runner. We have no reason to argue differently, but still, Landy's looking back as Bannister passed him is frozen in time forever and only took a moment. His looking back leaves one wondering what would have happened if he just focused on the finish line.

I was so intrigued by this story I did some in depth reading on competitive running. I learned that serious runners conclude that looking back is a serious distraction. What seems like a momentary minor choice can have a huge impact on one's mental ability to successfully complete a race. They surmise that looking back interrupts momentum and form. One highly experienced athlete commented that looking back changes her focus from one of running to win to one of running to avoid losing.

With the phrase "looking back" on top of mind, I contemplated the words of the Apostle Paul to the church in Philippi: "Forgetting the past and looking forward to what lies ahead, I strain to reach the end of the race and receive the prize for which God is calling us up to heaven because of what Christ Jesus did for us (Philippians 3:13-14, Living Bible)." What wise counsel is there at the intersection of the Miracle Mile story and Paul's words to believers about his walk of faith? Ironically, both speak to us from the past. As a history buff, I constantly look back in order to learn life lessons for the present and future. Clearly there are different types of looking back, and there is value in it as a history enthusiast, as a disciple of Jesus or simply as one seeking to understand the past in order to live life better in the present and the future. Today my musings are particularly around looking back over one's own personal life history. When it comes to 'weighing' my past, the following three maxims are helpful:

- Those who do not know history are doomed to repeat it.
- Don't look back, you're not going that way.
- All things in good measure.

As a disciple of Jesus, I must also heed the teaching of Jesus about serving him and looking back:

> "No one who put his hand to the plow and looks back
> is fit for the service in the kingdom of God."
> Luke 9:62 NIV

As I navigate this matter of "looking back" concerning my own life, here are some things I've learned:

Looking back can result in HEALTHY outcomes:

- increasing confidence, faith, and peace;
- reminding yourself of past blessings;
- learning from failures so as not to repeat them;
- learning from victories so as to repeat them; and,
- confronting unhealthy or sinful behaviours to be vanquished transformed, confessed, etc.

Letter Forty-Eight

Here I tell myself: *Look back to learn but focus forward to live.*

Looking back can result in UNHEALTHY outcomes:

- fostering doubt, anxiety, and fear;
- fostering bitterness or a desire for revenge;
- justifying present destructive behaviour;
- punishing yourself (or others) for past failures;
- avoiding present or future realities; and,
- avoiding the making of decisions about the present or future.

Here I tell myself: *Don't look back; you don't want to go that way.*

So much more can be said here, but let me leave you with some final thoughts about discipleship and the practice of looking back over your own life experiences: Who you used to be is not as important as who God calls you to be in the present and future. What you have done is also not as important as what God calls you to do in the present and future. Above all, as a disciple, always fix your eyes on Jesus. He is the same yesterday, today and forever (Hebrews 12:2; 13:8).

Be blessed, my friends.

Letters to my Friends

REFLECTIONS

LETTER FORTY-NINE

Sabbath

Letters to my Friends

Hello Friends.

"Because of the Lord's great love we are not consumed, for his compassions never fail. They are new every morning; great is your faithfulness" (Lamentations 3:22-23). *So God, It's A New Day* was written in Saskatoon, Saskatchewan on May 5, 2012.

SO GOD, IT'S A NEW DAY

So God, it's a new day.
And yet, I'm not sure I'm set.
I tether my trust to you; I cinch it tight.
I adorn my soul with divine armor: truth, righteousness, peace,
    faith, salvation and the Spirit's sword.
Aware of this day's fount of follies and fortunes, I step out,
    guarded in heart but sanguine in spirit.
The course before me virgin, no foot-worn path as compass,
    what trials await encounter, what temptations
    loom ahead?
Will trust in you be tested, hope tried?
Will doubt best me, indifference beguile?
And of the pace, should I tarry or make haste, linger or bound on?
What divine appointments are scripted; interruptions ordained?
O God, I pray wisdom to navigate the moments, discernment
    to chart the hours.
And, when dark-fall broaches, I sense on my account,
    heaven's vault was accessed.
A portion of God's treasured grace was poured upon me for
    the sojourn, and it sufficed.

*Heartwork – Grace Like Rain, PG, 2012.

Letter Forty-Nine

SABBATH PRAYER

Hello Friends.

On April 11, 1999, I felt blessed to finish a prayer residing in my heart – . This prayer is based upon Psalm 45 and was birthed out of a life-transforming worship experience and written for a corporate worship setting.

"Let everything that has breath, praise the Lord. Praise the Lord"
Psalm 150:6

Look back and trust Him.
Look ahead and trust Him.
Look around and serve Him.
Look up and expect Him.
Author unknown

PRAYER OF PRAISE

Our gracious Redeemer, may we this morning echo the words of
    the Psalmist who proclaimed, *"Great is the Lord, and*
    highly to be praised...the Lord is gracious and merciful; slow
    to anger and great in loving-kindness."
May we, Lord God, offer unto you this morning a song
    celebrating your faithfulness in our lives.
May we herald the power of your name and the awesome
    wonder of your majesty.
May we, Lord God, re-commit ourselves to sincere worship
    of you.

Accept our worship this morning.
May it be a sweet fragrance of praise in your sight.
May we kneel before you and shout with every fiber of our being
    that you are the King of kings and Lord of lords
    and God of gods.
Amen.

Heartwork – An Endless Hallelujah, PG, 2011.

Letter Forty-Nine

REFLECTIONS

VALEDICTION

> "For the Lord your God is living among you. He is a mighty savior. He will take delight in you with gladness. With his love, he will calm all your fears. He will rejoice over you with joyful songs."
> Zephaniah 3:17 NLT

The final words of any letter seem to be the hardest. The task is even more challenging when it is to be the valediction on forty-two letters. One wants to express the most memorable sentiment at the end, right? Well, after considerable thought, and some inspiration from the Holy Spirit, I want to share a full-on encouragement.

In Christ, you are the Father's beloved, and as such, genuinely worthy to receive the profound riches of His grace, forgiveness, love, hope, peace and joy. The Father is poised to shower upon you all that you need to live life to the fullest. Hold tightly to the declaration of the Apostle Paul to the church in Philippi: "And my God will meet all your needs according to his glorious riches

Valediction

in Christ Jesus" (Philippians 4:19). We can do amazing things in this life because of God's presence and blessings.

In this life we will have many voices diminishing our faith in God's goodness, and our status as His beloved. I get that. I've heard these voices often throughout my ministry, some coming from people, some from our supernatural enemy, and some from my own heart. And so, as a departing encouragement in case you are feeling downhearted today:

You genuinely matter
   you're important
   you're worthy
   you're thought of
   you're blessed
   you're loved.
Today,
     your presence and voice
     on this earth make a difference
     whether you feel it or not.
Today,
     be encouraged
     be bold
     be confident
     be creative
     be a risk-taker
     be open to a miracle
     be Christ-like
     be still and know that God's got you, and this.

Be blessed, my friends.

NOTES

1. Philip Gunther, *Pilgrimage Journals* (unpublished).
2. Tod Bolsinger, *Tempered Resilience* (Downers Grove, Illinois: InterVarsity Press, 2020), p. 35.
3. Amit Sood, *Discover the Resilient You – Everyday Health Workbook* (Global Center for Resiliency and Wellbeing, unknown publication date), p.2.
4. https://www.goodreads.com/quotes/559181-a-good-half-of-the-art-of-living-is-resilience
5. Richard Foster, *Celebration Of Discipline* (San Francisco, California: Harper & Row Publishers, 1978), p. 6.
6. Andy Stanley, *Better Decisions, Fewer Regrets* (Grand Rapids, Michigan: Zondervan, 2020), p. 23.
7. http://www.eleanorbrownn.com/blog2/self-care-in-not-selfish
8. https://www.leadingwithhonor.com/leading-with-honor-wisdom-for-today-april-9-2021/
9. Viktor E. Frankl, *Man's Search for Meaning* (Boston, Massachusetts: Beacon Press, 1959, 1962, 1992, 2006), p. 76. Source of quote unknown.

10. https://decisionmagazine.com/
    putting-holes-in-the-darkness/
11. Philip Gunther, *Pilgrimage Journals* (unpublished).
12. L.B. Cowman, *Streams in the Desert* (Grand Rapids, Michigan: Zondervan, 1997), p. 135.
13. Kyle Idleman, *Not a Fan* (Grand Rapids, Michigan: Zondervan, 2011).
14. Henri Nouwen, *The Way of The Heart* (New York, New York: HarperOne, 1981), p.12.
15. Jerry Bridges, *The Practice of Godliness* (Colorado Springs, Colorado: NavPress, 1983, 1996), p. 16.
17. W.E. Vine, *Vine's Expository Dictionary of Old and New Testament Words* (Old Tappan, New Jersey: Fleming H. Revell Company, 1981), p. 162-163.
18. https://www.nobelprize.org/prizes/peace/1979/
    teresa/26200-mother-teresa-acceptance-speech-1979/
19. http://www.glenarmbaptistchurch.co.uk/
    quotes-jesus-influence-on-history/471
20. Viktor E. Frankl, *Man's Search For Meaning* (Boston, Massachusetts: Beacon Press, 1959, 1962, 1992, 2006), p. 65-66.
21. https://www.pepquotes.com/terry-goodkind-quotes
22. Walter Klassen, ed., *Anabaptism In Outline* (Kitchner, Ontario: Herald Press, 1981), p. 267.
23. Helen Adams Keller, *Helen Keller's Journal: 1936-1937* (New York, New York: Doubleday, Doran & company, Inc., 1938), p.60.
24. Richard Swenson, *A Minute of Margin* (Colorado Springs, Colorado: NavPress, 2003), p. R11.
25. Richard Swenson, *A Minute of Margin* (Colorado Springs, Colorado: NavPress, 2003), p. R147.

26. Richard Swenson, *A Minute of Margin* (Colorado Springs, Colorado: NavPress, 2003), p. R132.
27. Richard Swenson, *A Minute of Margin* (Colorado Springs, Colorado: NavPress, 2003), p. R19.
28. John Mark Comer, *The Ruthless Elimination of Hurry* (Colorado Springs, Colorado, 2019), p. 46.
29. John Mark Comer, *The Ruthless Elimination of Hurry* (Colorado Springs, Colorado, 2019), p. 23.
30. John Mark Comer, *The Ruthless Elimination of Hurry* (Colorado Springs, Colorado, 2019), p. 25.
31. Peter Scazzero, *Emotionally Healthy Spirituality* (Grand Rapids, Michigan: Zondervan, 2014, 2017).
32. Henry David Thoreau, *Walden* (Boston, Massachusetts: Ticknor and Fields, 1854).
33. Richard Swenson, *In Search of Balance* (Colorado Springs, Colorado: NavPress, 2010), p. 136.
34. Richard Swenson, *A Minute of Margin* (Colorado Springs, Colorado: NavPress, 2003), p. R116.
35. Richard Swenson, *Contentment: The Secret to a Lasting Calm* (Colorado Springs, Colorado: NavPress, 2013), p. 18.
36. Richard Swenson, *Contentment: The Secret to a Lasting Calm* (Colorado Springs, Colorado: NavPress, 2013), p. 52.
37. Philip Gunther, *Pilgrimage Journals* (unpublished).
38. https://www.fathersloveletter.com/fll_devotional_index.html
39. Thomas Watson, *The Art of Contentment: An Exposition of Philippians 4:11* (1653) – https://www.monergism.com/thethreshold/sdg/watson/TheArtofDivineContentmentThomasWatson.pdf
40. Thomas Watson, *The Art of Contentment: An Exposition of Philippians 4:11* (1653) – https://www.monergism.com/thethreshold/sdg/watson/

Notes

TheArtofDivineContentmentThomasWatson.pdf
41. Richard Swenson, Contentment: *The Secret to a Lasting Calm* (Colorado Springs, Colorado: NavPress, 2013), p. 197.
42. Jeremiah Burroughs, *The Rare Jewel of Christian Contentment* (Carlisle, Pennsylvania: The Banner of Truth Trust,1648), p. 4.
43. https://www.poetryfoundation.org/poems/44272/the-road-not-taken
44. https://www.azquotes.com/author/11496-William_Penn
45. J.C. Wenger, ed., *The Complete Writings of Menno Simons* c. 1496-1561 (Scottdale, Pennsylvania: Herald Press, 1956, 1984). 1871 version edited by John F. Funk:
46. http://www.mennosimons.net/completewritings.html
47. https://minimalistquotes.com/robin-williams-quote-6020/
48. https://www.goodreads.com/author/quotes/268964. Jesse_Jackson
49. Reggie McNeal, *A Work of Heart* (San Francisco, California: Jossey-Bass, 2000), p.185.
50. https://prts.edu/wp-content/uploads/2016/12/Shorter_Catechism.pdf
51. Dietrich Bonhoeffer, *The Cost of Discipleship* (New York, New York: Collier Books, 1937), p. 7.
52. Wilbur E. Rees, *$3 Worth of God* (Prussia, Pennsylvania: Judson Press, 1971).
53. Dietrich Bonhoeffer, *The Cost of Discipleship* (New York, New York: Macmillan Publishing Company, 1949), p. 47-48.
54. https://library.timelesstruths.org/music/When_I_Survey_the_Wondrous_Cross/
55. Henry and Richard Blackaby, *Encountering God Day By Day Devotional* (Nashville, Tennessee: Broadman & Holman, 1998), p.7,40.

56. Oswald Chambers, *My Utmost For His Highest* (Uhrichsville, Ohio: Barbour and Company, Inc., 1963), p.89.
57. Tremper Longman III, *How to Read Proverbs* (Downers Grove, Illinois: IVP Academic; 2002), p. 16.
58. https://www.wisdomhunters.com/what-is-wisdom/
59. Thomas Curtis Clark and Esther A. Gillespie, compilers, *1000 Quotable Poems* (New York: Harper & Brothers, 1937), p. 125.
60. Anthony Robbins, *Awaken the Giant Within* (New York, New York: Simon & Shuster; 1991), p. 376.
61. _____. The Oxford Dictionary of Quotations. Third Edition. Oxford: Oxford University Press; 1979, 296.
62. https://onlinelibrary.wiley.com/doi/abs/10.1111/1744-1633.12343
63. John MacArthur, *Our Sufficiency in Christ* (Wheaton, Illinois: Crossway Books, 1991), p.261.
64. https://www.poetseers.org/spiritual-and-devotional-poets/christian/teresa-of-avila/prayers-and-works/god-alone-is-enough/
65. Dallas Willard, *Renovation of the Heart: Putting on the Character of Christ* (Colorado Springs, Colorado: NavPress, 2002), 105.
66. Walter Klassen, ed., *Anabaptism in Outline* (Scottdale, Pennsylvania: Herald Press, 1981), 151.
67. Walter Klassen, ed., *Anabaptism in Outline* (Scottdale, Pennsylvania: Herald Press, 1981), 91.
68. Walter Klassen, ed., *Anabaptism in Outline* (Scottdale, Pennsylvania: Herald Press, 1981), 91.
69. https://www.youtube.com/watch?v=Owolr63y4Mw

Some of the unsourced supporting sentiments are borrowed. Unfortunately, however, at the time of writing some of the sources remain unidentified.

70. https://www.biography.com/athlete/wayne-gretzky

71. Henry Cloud, *Necessary Endings* (New York, New York: harper Business, 2010) p.63-64.
72. Hymn – *Make Me A Blessing*.
73. https://www.goodnewsnetwork.org/more/about-us/
74. *Protecting the Brain Against Bad News*. Canadian Medical Association Journal. Robin Blades. March 22, 2021. 193 (12) E428-E429. https://www.cmaj.ca/content/193/12/E428
75. *The Science Behind Doomscrolling*. ABC News. Benjamin Plackett. November 2020. https://abcnews.go.com/Technology/science-doomscrolling/story?id=74402415
76. *The Psychological Impact of Negative News*. Psychology Today. Graham C.L. Davey. September 21, 2020. https://www.psychologytoday.com/us/blog/why-we-worry/202009/the-psychological-impact-negative-news.
77. *You Asked: Is it Bad for You to Read the News Constantly?* Time. Markham Heid. May 19, 2020. https://time.com/5125894/is-reading-news-bad-for-you/
78. Jeffrey Kluger, *The Power Of Joy*, Time, November 13, 2020.
79. Eileen Daspin, "A Joyride Through History," November 13, 2020.
80. Theopathy – an emotional experience arising from religious belief.
81. Philip Gunther, *Pilgrimage Journals* (unpublished).
82. https://www.faiththeevidence.com/faith-evidence-blog-_1/whats-does-contentment-really-mean
83. C.S. Lewis, *Letters To Malcom: Chiefly on Prayer* (San Diego, California: Harvest, 1964), 93.
83. Carol McLeod, *Vibrant* (New Kensington, Pennsylvania: Whitaker House, 2020), p. 59-60.
84. https://www.azquotes.com/quote/555869
85. Jay Chaliha (compiler), *The Joy in Loving: A guide to Daily*

Living (London, England: Penguin Books, 2000).
86. https://henrinouwen.org/meditation/joy/
87. J.C. Wenger, ed., *The Complete Writings of Menno Simons* c. 1496-1561 (Scottdale, Pennsylvania: Herald Press, 1956, 1984), p.621. 1871 version edited by john F. Funk:
88. http://www.mennosimons.net/completewritings.html
89. https://www.goodreads.com/author/quotes/23041.John_Wooden?page=4
90. Rick Warren. *The Purpose Driven Life* (Grand Rapids, Michigan: Zondervan, 2002), 63.
91. Rick Warren. *The Purpose Driven Life* (Grand Rapids, Michigan: Zondervan, 2002), 37.
92. The Miracle Mile – 1954 – A Moment In Time. http://www.miraclemile1954.com

Notes

www.ingramcontent.com/pod-product-compliance
Lightning Source LLC
Chambersburg PA
CBHW062042080426
42734CB00012B/2535